OUT OF THE DARKNESS

Peter Ellison Short Stories for GCSE

Edward Arnold
A division of Hodder & Stoughton
LONDON BALTIMORE MELBOURNE AUCKLAND

Acknowledgments

The publishers would like to thank the following for their kind permission to reproduce copyright material in this book:

'The Darkness Out There' from *You Can't Keep Out the Darkness* (1980) by Penelope Lively, published by The Bodley Head and reprinted by permission of Murray Pollinger; 'A Stench of Kerosene' by Amrita Pritam from *Land of Five Rivers: Stories From the Punjab* (1965) reprinted by permission of the publishers, Jaico Publishing House, Bombay; 'Invisible Boy' from *Golden Apples of the Sun* (1977) by Ray Bradbury, published by Hart Davis Ltd and reprinted by permission of Abner Stein; 'Flight' from *A Habit of Loving* by Doris Lessing, published by MacGibbon & Kee Ltd, copyright © 1957 Doris Lessing, reprinted by permission of Jonathan Clowes Ltd, London; 'No Witchcraft for Sale' from *This Was the Old Chief's Country* by Doris Lessing, published by Michael Joseph Ltd, copyright © 1951 Doris Lessing, reprinted by permission of Jonathan Clowes Ltd, London; 'The Healing' by Dorothy Nimmo from *First Fictions Introduction 9*, published by Faber and Faber Ltd and reprinted by permission of the author; 'Revenge' from *In the Land of Dreamy Dreams* (1981) by Ellen Gilchrist, reprinted by permission of the publishers, Faber and Faber Ltd; 'The Conversion of the Jews' from *Goodbye Columbus* (1959) by Philip Roth, reprinted by permission of the publishers, André Deutsch Ltd; 'The Flashlight' from *Dear Baby* by William Saroyan, published by Faber & Faber Ltd and reprinted by permission of Laurence Pollinger Ltd and The William Saroyan Foundation; 'More than just the Disease' from *The Great Profundo and Other Stories* by Bernard MacLaverty, reprinted by permission of the publishers, Jonathan Cape Ltd.

Also available: *Out of the Darkness Students' Workbook* (0 7131 7811 6)

© 1988 Peter Ellison
First published in Great Britain 1988

British Cataloguing in Publication Data
Out of the darkness: short stories for
  GCSE.
  I. Ellison, Peter
  8213'.01'08[FS]

ISBN 0-7131-7810-8

All rights reserved. No part of this publication may be reproduced or transmitted in any form or by any means, electronically or mechanically, including photocopying, recording or any information storage or retrieval system, without either the prior permission in writing from the publisher or a licence permitting restricted copying. In the United Kingdom such licences are issued by the Copyright Licensing Agency, 33–34 Alfred Place, London WC1E 7DP.

Typeset in Linotron Palatino by Gecko Limited, Bicester, Oxon.
Printed and bound in Great Britain for Edward Arnold, the educational, academic and medical publishing division of Hodder and Stoughton Limited, Mill Road, Dunton Green, Sevenoaks, Kent by Richard Clay Ltd, Bungay, Suffolk

Contents

To the Teacher	iv
1 The Darkness Out There *Penelope Lively*	1
2 A Stench of Kerosene *Amrita Pritam*	14
3 Invisible Boy *Ray Bradbury*	19
4 Flight *Doris Lessing*	29
5 No Witchcraft for Sale *Doris Lessing*	35
6 The Healing *Dorothy Nimmo*	43
7 Revenge *Ellen Gilchrist*	47
8 The Conversion of the Jews *Philip Roth*	61
9 The Flashlight *William Saroyan*	77
10 More than just the Disease *Bernard MacLaverty*	80

To the Teacher

Out of the Darkness is an anthology of contemporary short stories which is built around the symbolic conflict between darkness and light. Most collections consist of stories grouped under a broad theme, the theory being that each of the stories is in some way 'about' whatever the title of the collection says. However, because the theme does not actually help students to reach a deeper understanding of the stories, teachers tend to use such anthologies for perhaps one or two stories only, by and large ignoring the theme altogether. The organisation of this anthology enables students to focus on the stories' symbolic structure and to build up their understanding of the structure of short stories as a whole, in a way that the more arbitrary grouping of thematic anthologies is less likely to do.

To gain the most from the arrangement of these stories, however, students will need the accompanying *Students' Workbook* which contains a wide variety of activities and written assignments (suitable for both language and literature work), which are designed to guide students to a deeper understanding of each story. For those students wanting to compare short stories for a coursework assignment, suggested structures are also provided.

1. The Darkness Out There

Penelope Lively

She walked through flowers, the girl, oxeye daisies and vetch and cow parsley, keeping to the track at the edge of the field. She could see the cottage in the distance, shrugged down into the dip beyond the next hedge. Mrs Rutter, Pat had said, Mrs Rutter at Nether Cottage, you don't know her, Sandra? She's a dear old thing, all on her own, of course, we try to keep an eye. A wonky leg after her op and the home help's off with a bad back this week. So could you make that your Saturday afternoon session, dear? Lovely. There'll be one of the others, I'm not sure who.

Pat had a funny eye, a squint, so that her glance swerved away from you as she talked. And a big chest jutting under washed-out jerseys. Are people who help other people always not very nice-looking? Very busy being busy; always in a rush. You didn't get people like Mrs Carpenter at the King's Arms running the Good Neighbours Club. People with platinum highlights and spike heel suede boots.

She looked down at her own legs, the girl, bare brown legs brushing through the grass, polleny summer grass that glinted in the sun.

She hoped it would be Susie, the other person. Or Liz. They could have a good giggle, doing the floors and that. Doing her washing, this old Mrs Rutter.

They were all in the Good Neighbours Club, her set at school. Quite a few of the boys, too. It had become a sort of craze, the thing to do. They were really nice, some of the old people. The old folks, Pat called them. Pat had done the notice in the Library: *Come and have fun giving a helping hand to the old folks. Adopt a granny.* And the joky cartoon drawing of a dear old bod with specs on the end of her nose and a shawl. One or two of the old people had been a bit sharp about that.

The track followed the hedge round the field to the gate and the plank bridge over the stream. The dark reach of the spinney came right to the gate there so that she would have to walk by the edge of it with the light suddenly shutting off, the bare wide sky of the field. Packer's end.

You didn't go by yourself through Packer's End if you could help it, not after tea-time, anyway. A German plane came down in the war and the aircrew were killed and there were people who'd heard them talking still, chattering in German on their radios, voices coming out of the trees, nasty, creepy. People said.

She kept to the track, walking in the flowers with corn running in the wind between her and the spinney. She thought suddenly of blank-eyed helmeted heads, looking at you from among branches. She wouldn't go in there for a thousand pounds, not even in bright day like now, with nothing coming out of the dark slab of trees but birdsong – blackbirds and thrushes and robins and that. It was a rank place, all whippy saplings and brambles and a gully with a dumped mattress and bedstead and an old fridge. And, somewhere, presumably, the crumbling rusty scraps of metal and cloth and . . . Bones?

It was all right out here in the sunshine. Fine. She stopped to pick grass stems out of her sandal; she saw the neat print of the strap-marks against her sunburn, pink-white on brown. Somebody had said she had pretty feet, once; she looked at them, clean and plump and neat on the grass. A ladybird crawled across a toe.

When they were small, six and seven and eight, they'd been scared stiff of Packer's End. Then, they hadn't known about the German plane. It was different things then; witches and wolves and tigers. Sometimes they'd go there for a dare, several of them, skittering over the field and into the edge of the trees, giggling and shrieking, not too far in, just far enough for it to be scary, for the branch shapes to look like faces and clawed hands, for the wolves to rustle and creep in the greyness you couldn't quite see into, the clotted shifting depths of the place.

But after, lying on your stomach at home on the hearthrug watching telly with the curtains drawn and the dark shut out it was cosy to think of Packer's End, where you weren't.

After they were twelve or so the witches and wolves went away. Then it was the German plane. And other things too. You didn't know who there might be around, in woods and places. Like stories in the papers.
Girl attacked on lonely road. Police hunt rapist. There was this girl, people at school said, this girl sometime back who'd been biking along the field path and these two blokes had come out of Packer's End, they'd had a knife, they'd threatened to carve her up, there wasn't anything she could do, she was at their mercy. People couldn't remember what her name was, exactly, she didn't live round here any more. Two enormous blokes, sort of gypsy types.

She put her sandal back on. She walked through the thicker grass by the hedge and felt it drag at her legs and thought of swimming in warm seas. She put her hand on the top of her head and her hair was hot from the sun, a dry burning cap. One day, this year, next year sometime, she would go to places like on travel brochures and run into a blue sea. She would fall in love and she would get a good job and she would have one of those new Singers that do zig-zag stitch and make an embroidered silk coat.

One day.

Now, she would go to this old Mrs Rutter's and have a bit of a giggle with Susie and come home for tea and wash her hair. She would walk like this through the silken grass with the wind seething the corn and the secret invisible life of birds beside her in the hedge. She would pick a blue flower and examine its complexity of pattern and petal and wonder what it was called and drop it. She would plunge her face into the powdery plate of an elderflower and smell cat, tom-cat, and sneeze and scrub her nose with the back of her hand. She would hurry through the gate and over the stream because that was a bit too close to Packer's End for comfort and she would . . .

He rose from the plough beyond the hedge.

She screamed.

'Christ!' she said. 'Kerry Stevens you stupid so-and-so, what d'you want to go and do that for you give me the fright of my life.'

He grinned. 'I seen you coming. Thought I might as well wait.'

Not Susie. Not Liz either. Kerry Stevens from Richmond Way. Kerry Stevens that none of her lot reckoned much on, with his black licked-down hair and slitty eyes. Some people you only have to look at to know they're not up to much.

'Didn't know you were in the Good Neighbours.'

He shrugged. They walked in silence. He took out an aero bar, broke off a bit, offered it. She said oh, thanks. They went chewing towards the cottage, the cottage where old Mrs Rutter with her wonky leg would be ever so pleased to see them because they were really sweet, lots of the old people. Ever so grateful the old poppets, was what Pat said, not that you'd put it quite like that yourself.

'Just give it a push, the door. It sticks, see. That's it.'

She seemed composed of circles, a cottage-loaf of a woman, with a face below which chins collapsed one into another, a creamy smiling pool of a face in which her eyes snapped and darted.

'Tea, my duck?' she said. 'Tea for the both of you? I'll put us a kettle on.'

The room was stuffy. It had a gaudy lino floor with the pattern rubbed away in front of the sink and round the table; the walls were cluttered with old calendars and pictures torn from magazines; there was a smell of cabbage. The alcove by the fireplace was filled with china ornaments: big-eyed flop-eared rabbits and beribboned kittens and flowery milkmaids and a pair of naked chubby children wearing daisy chains.

The woman hauled herself from a sagging armchair. She glittered at them from the stove, manoeuvring cups, propping herself against the draining-board. 'What's your names, then? Sandra and Kerry. Well, you're a pretty girl, Sandra, aren't you. Pretty as they come. There was – let me see, who was it? – Susie, last week. That's right, Susie.' Her eyes investigated, quick as mice. 'Put your jacket on the back of the door, dear, you won't want to get that messy. Still at school, are you?'

The boy said 'I'm leaving, July. They're taking me on at the garage, the Blue Star. I been helping out there on and off, before.'

Mrs Rutter's smiles folded into one another. Above them, her eyes examined him. 'Well, I expect that's good steady money if you'd nothing special in mind. Sugar?'

There was a view from the window out over a bedraggled garden with stumps of spent vegetables and a matted flowerbed and a square of shaggy grass. Beyond, the spinney reached up to the fence, a no-man's-land of willowherb and thistle and small trees, growing thicker and higher into the full density of woodland. Mrs Rutter said, 'Yes, you have a look out, aren't I lucky – right up beside the wood. Lovely it is in the spring, the primroses and that. Mind, there's not as many as there used to be.'

The girl said, 'Have you lived here for a long time?'

'Most of my life, dear. I came here as a young married woman, and that's a long way back, I can tell you. You'll be courting before long yourself, I don't doubt. Like bees round the honeypot, they'll be.'

The girl blushed. She looked at the floor, at her own feet, neat and slim and brown. She touched, secretly, the soft skin of her thigh; she felt her breasts poke up and out at the thin stuff of her top; she licked the inside of her teeth, that had only the one filling, a speck like a pin-head. She wished there was Susie to have a giggle with, not just Kerry Stevens.

The boy said, 'What'd you like us to do?'

His chin was explosive with acne; at his middle, his jeans yawned from his T-shirt, showing pale chilly flesh. Mrs Rutter said, 'I expect you're a nice strong boy, aren't you? I daresay you'd like to have a go at the grass with the old mower. Sandra can give this room a do, that would be nice, it's as much as I can manage to have a dust of the ornaments just now, I can't get down to the floor.'

When he had gone outside the girl fetched broom and mop and dustpan from a cupboard under the narrow stair. The cupboard, stacked with yellowing

newspapers, smelt of damp and mouse. When she
returned the old woman was back in the armchair,
a composite chintzy mass from which cushions oozed
and her voice flowed softly on. 'That's it, dear, you just
work round, give the corners a brush if you don't mind,
that's where the dust settles. Mind your pretty skirt, pull
it up a bit, there's only me to see if you're showing a
bit of bum. That's ever such a nice style, I expect your
mum made it, did she?'

The girl said, 'Actually I did.'

'Well now, fancy! You're a little dressmaker, too, are
you? I was good with my needle when I was younger,
my eyesight's past it now, of course. I made my own
wedding dress, ivory silk with lace insets. *A Vogue*
pattern it was, with a sweetheart neckline.'

The door opened. Kerry said, 'Where'll I put the
clippings?'

'There's the compost heap down the bottom, by the
fence. And while you're down there could you get some
sticks from the wood for kindling, there's a good lad.'

When he had gone she went on, 'That's a nice boy.
It's a pity they put that stuff on their hair these days,
sticky-looking. I expect you've got lots of boyfriends,
though, haven't you?'

The girl poked in a crack at a clump of fluff. 'I don't
really know Kerry that much.'

'Don't you, dear. Well, I expect you get all sorts, in
your club thing, the club that Miss Hammond runs.'

'The Good Neighbours. Pat, we call her.'

'She was down here last week. Ever such a nice
person. Kind. It's sad she never married.'

The girl said, 'Is that your husband in the photo,
Mrs Rutter?'

'That's right, dear. In his uniform. The Ox and Bucks.
After he got his stripes. He was a lovely man.'

She sat back on her heels, the dustpan on her
lap. The photo was yellowish, in a silver frame.
'Did he . . .?'

'Killed in the war, dear. Right at the start. He was
in one of the first campaigns, in Belgium, and he never
came back.'

The girl saw a man with a tooth-brush moustache, his
army cap slicing his forehead. 'That's terrible.'

'Tragic. There was a lot of tragedies in the war. It's nice it won't be like that for you young people nowadays. Touch wood, cross fingers. I like young people, I never had any children, it's been a loss, that, I've got a sympathy with young people.'

The girl emptied the dustpan into the bin outside the back door. Beyond the fence, she could see the bushes thrash and Kerry's head bob among them. She thought, rather him than me, but it's different for boys, for him anyway, he's not a nervy type, it's if you're nervy you get bothered about things like Packer's End.

She was nervy, she knew. Mum always said so.

Mrs Rutter was rummaging in a cupboard by her chair. 'Chocky? I always keep a few chockies by for visitors.' She brought out a flowered tin. 'There. Do you know, I've had this twenty years, all but. Look at the little cornflowers. And the daisies. They're almost real, aren't they?'

'Sweet,' said the girl.

'Take them out and see if what's-'is-name would like one?'

There was a cindery path down the garden, ending at a compost heap where eggshells gleamed among leaves and grassclippings. Rags of plastic fluttered from sticks in a bed of cabbages. The girl picked her way daintily, her toes wincing against the cinders. A place in the country. One day she would have a place in the country, but not like this. Sometime. A little white house peeping over a hill, with a stream at the bottom of a crisp green lawn and an orchard with old apple trees and a brown pony. And she would walk in the long grass in this orchard in a straw hat with these two children, a boy and a girl, children with fair shiny hair like hers, and there'd be this man.

She leaned over the fence and shouted, 'Hey . . .'

'What?'

She brandished the box.

He came up, dumping an armful of sticks. 'What's this for, then?'

'She said. Help yourself.'

He fished among the sweets, his fingers etched with dirt. 'I did a job on your dad's car last week. That blue Escort's his, isn't it?'

'Mmn.'

'July, I'll be starting full-time. When old Bill retires. With day-release at the tech.'

She thought of oily workshop floors, of the foetid undersides of cars. She couldn't stand the feel of dirt, if her hands were the least bit grubby she had to go and wash, a rim of grime under her nails could make her shudder. She said, 'I don't know how you can, all that muck.'

He fished for another chocolate. 'Nothing wrong with a bit of dirt. What you going to do, then?'

'Secretarial.'

Men didn't mind so much. At home, her dad did things like unblocking the sink and cleaning the stove; mum was the same as her, just the feel of grease and stuff made her squirm. They couldn't either of them wear anything that had a stain or a spot.

He said 'I don't go much on her.'

'Who?'

He waved towards the cottage.

'She's all right. What's wrong with her, then?'

He shrugged. 'I dunno. The way she talks and that.'

'She lost her husband,' said the girl. 'In the war.' She considered him, across the fence, over a chasm. Mum said boys matured later, in many ways.

'There's lots of people done that.'

She looked beyond him, into distances. 'Tragic, actually. Well, I'll go back and get on. She says can you see to her bins when you've got the sticks. She wants them carried down for the dustmen.'

Mrs Rutter watched her come in, glinting from the cushions. 'That's a good girl. Put the tin back in the cupboard, dear.'

'What would you like me to do now?'

'There's my little bit of washing by the sink. Just the personal things to rinse through. That would be ever so kind.'

The girl ran water into the basin. She measured in the soapflakes. She squeezed the pastel nylons, the floating sinuous tights. 'It's a lovely colour, that turquoise.'

'My niece got me that last Christmas. Nightie and a little jacket to go. I was telling you about my wedding dress. The material came from Macy's, eight yards. I

cut it on the cross, for the hang. Of course, I had
a figure then.' She heaved herself round in the chair.
'You're a lovely shape, Sandra. You take care you
stay that way.'

'I can get a spare tyre,' the girl said. 'If I'm
not careful.'

Outside, the bin lids rattled.

'I hope he's minding my edging. I've got lobelia
planted out along that path.'

'I love blue flowers.'

'You should see the wood in the spring, with the
bluebells. There's a place right far in where you get
lots coming up still. I used to go in there picking every
year before my leg started playing me up. Jugs and jugs
of them, for the scent. Haven't you ever seen them?'

The girl shook her head. She wrung out the clothes,
gathered up the damp skein. 'I'll put these on the
line, shall I?'

When she returned the boy was bringing in the filled
coal-scuttle and a bundle of sticks.

'That's it,' said Mrs Rutter. 'Under the sink, that's
where they go. You'll want to have a wash after that,
won't you. Put the kettle on, Sandra, and we'll top
up the pot.'

The boy ran his hands under the tap. His shirt clung
to his shoulder-blades, damp with sweat. He looked over
the bottles of detergent, the jug of parsley, the handful
of flowers tucked into a coronation mug. He said, 'Is
that the wood where there was that German plane came
down in the war?'

'Don't start on that,' said the girl. 'It gives me
the willies.'

'What for?'

'Scary.'

The old woman reached forward and prodded the fire.
'Put a bit of coal on for me, there's a good boy. What's
to be scared of? It's over and done with, good riddance
to bad rubbish.'

'It was there, then?'

'Shut up,' said the girl.

'Were you here?'

'Fill my cup up, dear, would you. I was here.
Me and my sister. My sister Dot. She's dead now,

two years. Heart. That was before she was married, of course, nineteen forty-two, it was.'

'Did you see it come down?'

She chuckled. 'I saw it come down all right.'

'What was it?' said the boy. 'Messerschmitt?'

'How would I know that, dear? I don't know anything about aeroplanes. Anyway, it was all smashed up by the time I saw it, you couldn't have told t'other from which.'

The girl's hand hovered, the tea-cup halfway to her mouth. She sipped, put it down. 'You *saw* it? Ooh, I wouldn't have gone anywhere near.'

'It would have been burning,' said the boy. 'It'd have gone up in flames.'

'There weren't any flames, it was just stuck there in the ground, end up, with mess everywhere. Drop more milk, dear, if you don't mind.'

The girl shuddered. 'I s'pose they'd taken the bodies away by then.'

Mrs Rutter picked out a tea-leaf with the tip of the spoon. She drank, patted the corner of her mouth delicately with a tissue. 'No, no, 'course not. There was no one else seen it come down. We'd heard the engine and you could tell there was trouble, the noise wasn't right, and we looked out and saw it come down smack in the trees. 'Course we hadn't the telephone so there was no ringing the police or the Warden at Clapton. Dot said we should maybe bike to the village but it was a filthy wet night, pouring cats and dogs, and fog too and we didn't know if it was one of ours or one of theirs, did we? So Dot said better go and have a look first.'

'But either way . . .' the boy began.

'We got our wellies on, and Dot had the big lantern, and we went off. It wasn't very far in. We found it quite quick and Dot grabbed hold of me and pointed and we saw one of the wings sticking up with the markings on and we knew it was one of theirs. We cheered, I can tell you.'

The boy stared at her over the rim of the cup, blank faced.

'Dot said bang goes some more of the bastards, come on let's get back into the warm and we just started back when we heard this noise.'

'Noise?'

'Sort of moaning.'

'Oh,' cried the girl. 'How awful, weren't they . . .'

'So we got up closer and Dot held the lantern so we could see and there was three of them, two in the front and they was dead, you could see that all right, one of them had his . . .'

The girl grimaced. 'Don't.'

Mrs Rutter's chins shook, the pink and creamy chins. 'Good job you weren't there, then, my duck. Not that we were laughing at the time, I can tell you, rain teaming down and a raw November night, and that sight under our noses. It wasn't pretty but I've never been squeamish, nor Dot neither. And then we saw the other one.'

'The other one?' said the boy warily.

'The one at the back. He was trapped, see, the way the plane had broken up. There wasn't any way he could get out.'

The girl stiffened. 'Oh, lor, you mean he . . .'

'He was hurt pretty bad. He was kind of talking to himself. Something about mutter, mutter . . . Dot said he's not going to last long, and a good job too, three of them that'll be. She'd been a VAD so she knew a bit about casualties, see.' Mrs Rutter licked her lips; she looked across at them, her eyes darting. 'Then we went back to the cottage.'

There was silence. The fire gave a heave and a sigh. 'You what?' said the boy.

'Went back inside. It was bucketing down, cats and dogs.'

The boy and girl sat quite still, on the far side of the table.

'That was eighteen months or so after my hubby didn't come back from Belgium.' Her eyes were on the girl; the girl looked away. 'Tit for tat, I said to Dot.'

After a moment she went on. 'Next morning it was still raining and blow me if the bike hadn't got a puncture. I said to Dot I'm not walking to the village in this, and that's flat, and Dot was running a bit of a temp, she had the 'flu or something coming on. I tucked her up warm and when I'd done the chores I went back in the wood, to have another look. He must have been a tough so-and-so, that Jerry, he was still mumbling away. It gave me a turn, I can tell you, I'd never imagined he'd last the night. I could see him better, in the day-time; he was bashed up pretty nasty. I'd thought he was an old bloke, too, but he wasn't. He'd have been twentyish, that sort of age.'

The boy's spoon clattered to the floor; he did not move.

'I reckon he may have seen me, not that he was in a state to take much in. He called out something. I thought, oh no, you had this coming to you, mate, there's a war on. You won't know that expression – it was what everybody said in those days. I thought, why should I do anything for you? Nobody did anything for my Bill, did they? I was a widow at thirty-nine. I've been on my own ever since.'

The boy shoved his chair back from the table.

'He must have been a tough bastard, like I said. He was still there that evening, but the next morning he was dead. The weather'd perked up by then and I walked to the village and got a message to the people at Clapton. They were ever so surprised; they didn't know there'd been a Jerry plane come down in the area at all. There were lots of people came to take bits for souvenirs, I had a bit myself but it's got mislaid, you tend to mislay things when you get to my age.'

The boy had got up. He glanced down at the girl. 'I'm going,' he said. 'Dunno about you, but I'm going.'

She stared at the lacy cloth on the table, the fluted china cup. 'I'll come too.'

'Eh?' said the old woman. 'You're off, are you? That was nice of you to see to my little jobs for me. Tell what's-'er'-name to send someone next week if she can, I like having someone young about the place, once in a while, I've got a sympathy with young people. Here – you're forgetting your pretty jacket, Sandra, what's the hurry? 'Bye then, my ducks, see you close my gate, won't you?'

The boy walked ahead, fast; the girl pattered behind him, sliding on the dry grass. At the gateway into the cornfield he stopped. He said, not looking at her, looking towards the furzy edge of the wood, 'Christ!'

The wood sat there in the afternoon sun. Wind stirred the trees. Birds sang. There were not, the girl realised, wolves or witches or tigers. Nor were there prowling blokes, gypsy type blokes. And there were not chattering ghostly voices. Somewhere there were some scraps of metal overlooked by people hunting for souvenirs.

The boy said, 'I'm not going near that old bitch again.' He leaned against the gate, clenching his fists on an iron rung; he shook slightly. 'I won't ever forget him, that poor sod.'

She nodded.

'Two bloody nights. Christ!'

And she would hear, she thought, always, for a long time anyway, that voice trickling on, that soft old woman's voice; would see a tin painted with cornflowers, pretty china ornaments.

'It makes you want to throw up,' he said. 'Someone like that.'

She couldn't think of anything to say. He had grown; he had got older and larger. His anger eclipsed his acne, the patches of grease on his jeans, and lardy midriff. You could get people all wrong, she realised with alarm. You could get people wrong and there was a darkness that was not the darkness of tree shadows and murky undergrowth and you could not draw the curtains and keep it out because it was in your head, once known, in your head for ever like lines from a song. One moment you were walking in long grass with the sun on your hair and birds singing and the next you glimpsed darkness, an inescapable darkness. The darkness was out there and it was a part of you and you would never be without it, ever.

She walked behind him, through a world grown unreliable, in which flowers sparkle and birds sing but everything is not as it appears, oh no.

2. A Stench of Kerosene

Amrita Pritam

Outside, a mare neighed. Guleri recognised the neighing and ran out of the house. The mare was from her parents' village. She put her head against its neck as if it were the door to her father's house.

Guleri's parents lived in Chamba. A few miles from her husband's village which was on high ground, the road curved and descended steeply downhill. From this point one could see Chamba lying a long way away at one's feet. Whenever Guleri was homesick she would take her husband, Manak, and go up to this point. She would see the homes of Chamba twinkling in the sunlight and would come back, her heart glowing with pride.

Once every year, after the harvest had been gathered in, Guleri was allowed to spend a few days with her parents. They sent a man to Lakarmandi to bring her back to Chamba. Two of her friends, who were also married to boys who lived away from Chamba, came home at the same time and the girls looked forward to their annual reunion, talking about their joys and sorrow. They went about the streets together. Then there was the harvest festival when the girls would have new clothes made for the occasion. Their *dupattas* would be dyed, starched and sprinkled with mica to make them glisten. They would buy glass bangles and silver ear-rings.

Guleri always counted the days to the harvest. When autumn breezes cleared the skies of monsoon clouds, she thought of little else. She went about her daily chores – fed the cattle, cooked food for her parents-in-law – and then sat back to work out how long it would be before someone came to fetch her from her parents' village.

And now, once again, it was time for her annual visit. She caressed the mare joyfully, greeted her father's servant, Natu, and made preparations to leave the next day. She did not have to express her excitement in words; the look on her face was enough. Her husband pulled at his *hookah* and closed his eyes. It seemed as if he either did not like the tobacco or that he could not bear to face his wife.

'You'll come to the fair at Chamba, won't you? Come even for a day,' she pleaded.

Manak put aside his *chillum* but did not reply. 'Why don't you answer me?' she asked, a little cross. 'Shall I tell you something?'

'I know what you're going to say – that you only go to your parents once a year. Well you've never been stopped before.'

'Then why do you want to stop me this time?' she demanded.

'Just this once,' he pleaded.

'Your mother's said nothing so why do you stand in the way?' Guleri was childishly stubborn.

'My mother . . .' Manak did not finish his sentence.

On the long-awaited morning, Guleri was ready long before dawn. She had no children and therefore no problem of having to leave them behind or take them with her. Natu saddled the mare as she took leave of Manak's parents. They patted her head and blessed her.

'I'll come with you for part of the way,' Manak said.

Guleri was happy as they set out. She hid Manak's flute under her *dupatta*.

After the village of Khajiar, the road descended steeply to Chamba. There she took out the flute and gave it to him. She took his hand in hers and said, 'Come now, play your flute.' But Manak, lost in his thoughts, paid no heed. 'Why don't you play your flute?' she asked, coaxing him. He looked at her sadly. Then putting the flute to his lips, blew a strange anguished wail.

'Guleri, don't go away,' he begged her. 'I ask again, don't go away this time.' He handed the flute to her, unable to continue.

'But why?' she asked. 'Come over on the day of the fair and we'll return together, I promise you.'

Manak did not ask again.

They stopped by the roadside. Natu took the mare a few paces ahead to leave the couple alone. It crossed Manak's mind that it was at this time of the year, seven years ago, that he and his friends had come on this very road to go to the harvest festival in Chamba. And it was at this fair that

Manak had first seen Guleri and they had bartered their hearts to each other. Later, managing to meet her alone, he remembered taking her hand and telling her, 'You are like unripe corn – full of milk.'

'Cattle go for unripe corn,' Guleri had replied, freeing her hand with a jerk. 'Human beings prefer it roasted. If you want me, go and ask my father for my hand.'

Among Manak's kinsmen it was customary to settle the bride price before the wedding. Manak was nervous because he did not know the price Guleri's father would demand from him. But Guleri's father was prosperous and had lived in cities. He had sworn that he would not take money for his daughter but would give her to a worthy young man from a good family. Manak, he decided, answered these requirements and soon after, Guleri and Manak were married. Deep in memories, Manak was roused by Guleri's hand on his shoulder.

'What are you dreaming of?' she teased him.

He did not answer. The mare neighed impatiently and Guleri got up to leave. 'Do you know the bluebell wood a couple of miles from here?' she asked. 'It's said that anyone who goes through it becomes deaf. You must have passed through that bluebell wood. You don't seem to be hearing anything I say.'

'You're right, Guleri. I can't hear anything you're saying to me,' and Manak sighed.

They looked at each other. Neither understood the other's thoughts. 'I'll go now,' Guleri said gently. 'You'd better go back. You've come a long way from home.'

'You've walked all the distance. You'd better get on the mare,' replied Manak.

'Here, take your flute.'

'You take it.'

'Will you come and play it on the day of the fair?' she asked with a smile. The sun shone in her eyes. Manak turned his face away. Perplexed, Guleri shrugged her shoulders and took the road to Chamba. Manak returned home.

He entered the house and slumped listlessly on the *charpoy*. 'You've been away a long time,' exclaimed his mother. 'Did you go all the way to Chamba?'

'Not all the way, only to the top of the hill.' Manak's voice was heavy.

'Why do you croak like an old woman?' said his mother severely. 'Be a man.'

Manak wanted to retort, 'You are a woman; why don't you cry like one for a change!' But he remained silent.

Manak and Guleri had been married seven years but she had never borne a child and Manak's mother had made a secret resolve that she would not let it go beyond the eighth year. This year, true to her decision, she had paid five hundred *rupees* to get him a second wife and she was waiting, as Manak knew, for Guleri to go to her parents before bringing in the new bride. Obedient to his mother and to custom, Manak's body responded to the new woman but his heart was dead within him.

In the early hours one morning he was smoking his *chillum* when an old friend happened to pass by. 'Ho, Bhavani, where are you going so early in the morning?'

Bhavani stopped. He had a small bundle on his shoulder. 'Nowhere in particular,' he said evasively.

'You should be on your way to some place or the other,' exclaimed Manak. 'What about a smoke?'

Bhavani sat down on his haunches and took the chillum from Manak's hands. 'I'm going to Chamba for the fair,' he said at last.

Bhavani's words pierced through Manak's heart like a needle. 'Is the fair today?'

'It's the same day, every year,' replied Bhavani drily. 'Don't you remember, we were in the same party seven years ago?' Bhavani did not say any more but Manak was conscious of the other man's rebuke and he felt uneasy. Bhavani put down the chillum and picked up his bundle. His flute was sticking out of the bundle. Manak's eye remained on the flute till Bhavani disappeared from view.

Next morning, Manak was in his fields when he saw Bhavani coming back but he looked the other way deliberately. He did not want to talk to Bhavani to hear anything about the fair. But Bhavani came round the other side and sat down in front of Manak. His face was sad and grey as a cinder.

'Guleri is dead,' Bhavani said in a flat voice.

'What?'

'When she heard of your second marriage, she soaked her clothes in kerosene and set fire to them.'

Manak, mute with pain, could only stare and feel his own life burning out.

The days went by. Manak resumed his work in the fields and ate his meals when they were given to him. But he was like a dead man, his face blank, his eyes empty.

'I am not his wife,' complained his second wife. 'I'm just someone he happened to marry.'

But quite soon she was pregnant and Manak's mother was pleased with her new daughter-in-law. She told Manak about his wife's condition, but he looked as if he did not understand and his eyes were still empty.

His mother encouraged her daughter-in-law to bear with her husband's moods for a few days. As soon as the child was born and placed in his father's lap, she said, Manak would change.

A son was duly born to Manak's wife; and his mother, rejoicing, bathed the boy, dressed him in fine clothes and put him in Manak's lap. Manak stared at the new-born babe in his lap. He stared a long time, uncomprehending, his face as usual expressionless. Then suddenly the blank eyes filled with horror and Manak began to scream. 'Take him away!' he shrieked hysterically, 'Take him away! He stinks of kerosene.'

3. Invisible Boy

Ray Bradbury

She took the great iron spoon and the mummified frog and gave it a bash and made dust of it, and talked to the dust while she ground it in her stony fists quickly. Her beady gray bird-eyes flickered at the cabin. Each time she looked, a head in the small thin window ducked as if she'd fired off a shotgun.

'Charlie!' cried Old Lady. 'You come outa there! I'm fixing a lizard magic to unlock that rusty door You come out now and I won't make the earth shake or the trees go up in fire or the sun set at high noon!'

The only sound was the warm mountain light on the high turpentine trees, a tufted squirrel chittering around and around on a green-furred log, the ants moving in a fine brown line at Old Lady's bare, blue-veined feet.

'You been starving in there two days, darn you!' she panted, chiming the spoon against a flat rock, causing the plump gray miracle bag to swing at her waist. Sweating sour, she rose and marched at the cabin, bearing the pulverized flesh. 'Come out, now!' She flicked a pinch of powder inside the lock. 'All right, I'll come get you!' she wheezed.

She spun the knob with one walnut-colored hand, first one way, then the other. 'O Lord,' she intoned, 'fling this door wide!'

When nothing flung, she added yet another philter and held her breath. Her long blue untidy skirt rustled as she peered into her bag of darkness to see if she had any scaly monsters there, any charm finer than the frog she'd killed months ago for such a crisis as this.

She heard Charlie breathing against the door. His folks had pranced off into some Ozark town early this week, leaving him, and he'd run almost six miles to Old Lady for company – she was by way of being an aunt or cousin or some such, and he didn't mind her fashions.

But then, two days ago, Old Lady, having gotten used to the boy around, decided to keep him for convenient company. She pricked her thin shoulder bone, drew out three blood pearls, spat wet over her right elbow, tramped on a crunch-cricket, and at the same instant clawed her left hand at Charlie, crying, 'My son you are, you are my son, for all eternity!'

Charlie, bounding like a startled hare, had crashed off into the bush, heading for home.

But Old Lady, skittering quick as a gingham lizard, cornered him in a dead end, and Charlie holed up in this old hermit's cabin and wouldn't come out, no matter how she whammed door, window, or knothole with amber-colored fist or trounced her ritual fires, explaining to him that he was certainly her son *now*, all right.

'Charlie, you *there?*' she asked, cutting holes in the door planks with her bright little slippery eyes.

'I'm all of me here,' he replied finally, very tired.

Maybe he would fall out on the ground any moment. She wrestled the knob hopefully. Perhaps a pinch too much frog powder had grated the lock wrong. She always overdid or underdid her miracles, she mused angrily, never doing them just *exact*, Devil take it!

'Charlie, I only wants someone to night-prattle to, someone to warm hands with at the fire. Someone to fetch kindling for me mornings, and fight off the spunks that come creeping of early fogs! I ain't got no fetchings on you for myself, son, just for your company.' She smacked her lips. 'Tell you what, Charles, you come out and I *teach* you things!'

'What things?' he suspicioned.

'Teach you how to buy cheap, sell high. Catch a snow weasel, cut off its head, carry it warm in your hind pocket. There!'

'Aw,' said Charlie.

She made haste. 'Teach you to make yourself shotproof. So if anyone bangs at you with a gun, nothing happens.'

When Charlie stayed silent, she gave him the secret in a high fluttering whisper. 'Dig and stitch mouse-ear roots on Friday during full moon, and wear 'em around your neck in a white silk.'

'You're *crazy*,' Charlie said.

'Teach you how to stop blood or make animals stand frozen or make blind horses see, all them things I'll teach you! Teach you to cure a swelled-up cow and unbewitch a goat. Show you how to make yourself invisible!'

'Oh,' said Charlie.

Old Lady's heart beat like a Salvation tambourine.

The knob turned from the other side.

'You,' said Charlie, 'are funning me.'

'No, I'm not,' exclaimed Old Lady. 'Oh, Charlie, why, I'll make you like a window, see right through you. Why, child, you'll be surprised!'

'Real invisible?'

'Real invisible!'

'You won't fetch onto me if I walk out?'

'Won't touch a bristle of you, son.'

'Well,' he drawled reluctantly, 'all right.'

The door opened. Charlie stood in his bare feet, head down, chin against chest. 'Make me invisible,' he said.

'First we got to catch us a bat,' said Old Lady. 'Start lookin'!'

She gave him some jerky beef for his hunger and watched him climb a tree. He went high up and high up and it was nice seeing him there and it was nice having him here and all about after so many years alone with nothing to say good morning to but bird-droppings and silvery snail tracks.

Pretty soon a bat with a broken wing fluttered down out of the tree. Old Lady snatched it up, beating warm and shrieking between its porcelain white teeth, and Charlie dropped down after it, hand upon clenched hand, yelling.

That night, with the moon nibbling at the spiced pine cones, Old Lady extracted a long silver needle from under her wide blue dress. Gumming her excitement and secret anticipation, she sighted up the dead bat and held the cold needle steady-steady.

She had long ago realized that her miracles, despite all perspirations and salts and sulphurs, failed. But she had always dreamt that one day the miracles might start functioning, might spring up in crimson flowers and silver stars to prove that God had forgiven her for her pink body and her pink thoughts and her warm body and her warm thoughts as a young miss. But so far God had made no sign and said no word, but nobody knew this except Old Lady.

'Ready?' she asked Charlie, who crouched cross-kneed, wrapping his pretty legs in long goose-pimpled arms, his mouth open, making teeth. 'Ready,' he whispered, shivering.

'There!' She plunged the needle deep in the bat's right eye. 'So!'

'Oh!' screamed Charlie, wadding up his face.

'Now I wrap it in gingham, and here, put it in your pocket, keep it there, bat and all. Go on!'

He pocketed the charm.

'Charlie!' she shrieked fearfully. 'Charlie, where *are* you? I can't *see* you, child!'

'Here!' He jumped so the light ran in red streaks up his body. 'I'm here, Old Lady!' He stared wildly at his arms, legs, chest, and toes. 'I'm here!'

Her eyes looked as if they were watching a thousand fire-flies crisscrossing each other in the wild night air.

'Charlie, oh, you went *fast!* Quick as a hummingbird! Oh, Charlie, come *back* to me!'

'But I'm *here!*' he wailed.

'Where?'

'By the fire, the fire! And – and I can see myself. I'm not invisible at all!'

Old Lady rocked on her lean flanks. 'Course *you* can see *you!* Every invisible person knows himself. Otherwise, how could you eat, walk, or get around places? Charlie, touch me. Touch me so I *know* you.'

Uneasily he put out a hand.

She pretended to jerk, startled, at his touch. 'Ah!'

'You mean to say you can't *find* me?' he asked. 'Truly?'

'Not the least half rump of you!'

She found a tree to stare at, and stared at it with shining eyes, careful not to glance at him. 'Why, I sure *did* a trick *that* time!' She sighed with wonder. 'Whooeee. Quickest invisible I *ever* made! Charlie. Charlie, how you *feel?*'

'Like creek water – all stirred.'

'You'll settle.'

Then after a pause she added, 'Well, what you going to do now, Charlie, since you're invisible?'

All sorts of things shot through his brain, she could tell. Adventures stood up and danced like hell-fire in his eyes, and his mouth, just hanging, told what it meant to be a boy who imagined himself like the mountain winds. In a cold dream he said, 'I'll run across wheat fields, climb snow mountains, steal white chickens off'n farms. I'll kick pink pigs when they ain't looking. I'll pinch pretty girls' legs when they sleep, snap their garters in schoolrooms.' Charlie looked at Old Lady, and from the shiny tips of her eyes she saw something wicked shape his face. 'And other things I'll do, I'll do, I will,' he said.

'Don't try nothing on me,' warned Old Lady. 'I'm brittle as spring ice and I don't take handling.' Then: 'What about your folks?'

'My folks?'

'You can't fetch yourself home looking like that. Scare the inside ribbons out of them. Your mother'd faint straight back like timber falling. Think they want you about the house to stumble over and your ma have to call you every three minutes, even though you're in the room next her elbow?'

Charlie had not considered it. He sort of simmered down and whispered out a little 'Gosh' and felt of his long bones carefully.

'You'll be mighty lonesome. People looking through you like a water glass, people knocking you aside because they didn't reckon you to be underfoot. And women, Charlie, *women* ——'

He swallowed. 'What about women?'

'No woman will be giving you a second stare. And no woman wants to be kissed by a boy's mouth they can't even *find!*'

Charlie dug his bare toe in the soil contemplatively. He pouted. 'Well, I'll stay invisible, anyway, for a spell. I'll have me some fun. I'll just be pretty careful, is all. I'll stay out from in front of wagons and horses and Pa. Pa shoots at the nariest sound.' Charlie blinked. 'Why, with me invisible, someday Pa might just up and fill me with buckshot, thinkin' I was a hill squirrel in the dooryard. Oh . . .'

Old Lady nodded at a tree. 'That's likely.'

'Well,' he decided slowly, 'I'll stay invisible for tonight, and tomorrow you can fix me back all whole again, Old Lady.'

'Now if that ain't just like a critter, always wanting to be what he can't be,' remarked Old Lady to a beetle on a log.

'What you mean?' said Charlie.

'Why,' she explained, 'it was real hard work, fixing you up. It'll take a little *time* for it to wear off. Like a coat of paint wears off, boy.'

'You!' he cried. 'You did this to me! Now you make me back, you make me seeable!'

'Hush,' she said. 'It'll wear off, a hand or a foot at a time.'

'How'll it look, me around the hills with just one hand showing!'

'Like a five-winged bird hopping on the stones and bramble.'

'Or a foot showing!'

'Like a small pink rabbit jumping thicket.'

'Or my head floating!'

'Like a hairy balloon at a carnival!'

'How long before I'm *whole?*' he asked.

She deliberated that it might pretty well be an entire year.

He groaned. He began to sob and bite his lips and make fists. 'You magicked me, you did this, you did this thing to me. Now I won't be able to run home!'

She winked. 'But you *can* stay here, child, stay on with me real comfort-like, and I'll keep you fat and saucy.'

He flung it out: 'You did this on purpose! You mean old hag, you want to keep me here!'

He ran off through the shrubs on the instant.

'Charlie, come back!'

No answer but the pattern of his feet on the soft dark turf, and his wet choking cry which passed swiftly off and away.

She waited and then kindled herself a fire. 'He'll be back,' she whispered. And thinking inward on herself, she said, 'And now I'll have me my company through spring and into late summer. Then, when I'm tired of him and want a silence, I'll send him home.'

Charlie returned noiselessly with the first gray of dawn, gliding over the rimed turf to where Old Lady sprawled like a bleached stick before the scattered ashes.

He sat on some creek pebbles and stared at her.

She didn't dare look at him or beyond. He had made no sound, so how could she know he was anywhere about? She couldn't.

He sat there, tear marks on his cheeks.

Pretending to be just waking – but she had found no sleep from one end of the night to the other – Old Lady stood up, grunting and yawning, and turned in a circle to the dawn.

'Charlie?'

Her eyes passed from pines to soil, to sky, to the far hills. She called out his name, over and over again, and she felt like staring plumb straight at him, but she stopped herself. 'Charlie? Oh, Charles!' she called, and heard the echoes say the very same.

He sat, beginning to grin a bit, suddenly, knowing he was close to her, yet she must feel alone. Perhaps he felt the growing of a secret power, perhaps he felt secure from the world, certainly he was *pleased* with his invisibility.

She said aloud, 'Now where *can* that boy be? If he only made a noise so I could tell just where he is, maybe I'd fry him a breakfast.'

She prepared the morning victuals, irritated at his continuous quiet. She sizzled bacon on a hickory stick. 'The smell of it will draw his nose,' she muttered.

While her back was turned he swiped all the frying bacon and devoured it hastily.

She whirled, crying out, 'Lord!'

She eyed the clearing suspiciously. 'Charlie, that *you?*'

Charlie wiped his mouth clean on his wrists.

She trotted about the clearing, making like she was trying to locate him. Finally, with a clever thought, acting blind, she headed straight for him, groping. 'Charlie, where *are* you?'

A lightning streak, he evaded her, bobbing, ducking.

It took all her will power not to give chase; but you can't chase invisible boys, so she sat down, scowling, sputtering, and tried to fry more bacon. But every fresh strip she cut he would steal bubbling off the fire and run away far. Finally, cheeks burning, she cried, 'I know where you are! Right *there!* I hear you run!' She pointed to one side of him, not too accurate. He ran again, 'Now you're there!' she shouted. 'There, and there' pointing to all the places he was in the next five minutes. 'I hear you press a grass blade, knock a flower, snap a twig. I got fine shell ears, delicate as roses. They can hear the stars moving!'

Silently he galloped off among the pines, his voice trailing back, 'Can't hear me when I'm set on a rock. I'll just *set!*'

All day he sat on an observatory rock in the clear wind, motionless and sucking his tongue.

Old Lady gathered wood in the deep forest, feeling his eyes weaseling on her spine. She wanted to babble: 'Oh, I see you, I see you! I was only fooling about invisible boys! You're right there!' But she swallowed her gall and gummed it tight.

The following morning he did the spiteful thing. He began leaping from behind trees. He made toad-faces, frog-faces, spider-faces at her, clenching down his lips with his fingers, popping his raw eyes, pushing up his nostrils so you could peer in and see his brain thinking.

Once she dropped her kindling. She pretended it was a blue jay startled her.

He made a motion as if to strangle her.

She trembled a little.

He made another move as if to bang her shins and spit on her cheek.

These motions she bore without a lid-flicker or a mouth-twitch.

He stuck out his tongue, making strange bad noises. He wiggled his loose ears so she wanted to laugh, and finally she did laugh and explained it away quickly by saying, 'Sat on a salamander! Whew, how it poked!'

By high noon the whole madness boiled to a terrible peak.

For it was at that exact hour that Charlie came racing down the valley stark boy-naked!

Old Lady nearly fell flat with shock!

'Charlie!' she almost cried.

Charlie raced naked up one side of a hill and naked down the other – naked as a day, naked as the moon, raw as the sun and a newborn chick, his feet shimmering and rushing like the wings of a low-skimming hummingbird.

Old Lady's tongue locked in her mouth. What could she say? Charlie, go dress? For *shame? Stop* that? *Could* she? Oh, Charlie, Charlie, God! Could she say that now? *Well?*

Upon the big rock, she witnessed him dancing up and down, naked as the day of his birth, stomping bare feet, smacking his hands on his knees and sucking in and out his white stomach like blowing and deflating a circus balloon.

She shut her eyes tight and prayed.

After three hours of this she pleaded, 'Charlie, Charlie, come here! I got something to *tell* you!'

Like a fallen leaf he came, dressed again, praise the Lord.

'Charlie,' she said, looking at the pine trees, 'I see your right toe. *There* it is.'

'You do?' he said.

'Yes,' she said very sadly. 'There it is like a horny toad on the grass. And there, up there's your left ear hanging on the air like a pink butterfly.'

Charlie danced. 'I'm forming in, I'm forming in!'

Old Lady nodded. 'Here comes your ankle!'

'Gimme *both* my feet!' ordered Charlie.

'You got 'em.'

'How about my hands?'

'I see one crawling on your knee like a daddy longlegs.'

'How about the other one?'

'It's crawling too.'

'I got a body?'

'Shaping up fine.'

'I'll need my head to go home, Old Lady.'

To go home, she thought wearily. 'No!' she said, stubborn and angry. 'No, you ain't got no head. No head at all,' she cried. She'd leave that to the very last. 'No head, no head,' she insisted.

'No head?' he wailed.

'Yes, oh my God, yes, yes, you got your blamed head!' she snapped, giving up. 'Now fetch me back my bat with the needle in his eye!'

He flung it at her. 'Haaaa-yoooo!' His yelling went all up the valley, and long after he had run toward home she heard his echoes, racing.

Then she plucked up her kindling with a great dry weariness and started back toward her shack, sighing, talking. And Charlie followed her all the way, *really* invisible now, so she couldn't see him, just hear him, like a pine cone dropping or a deep underground stream trickling, or a squirrel clambering a bough; and over the fire at twilight she and Charlie sat, him so invisible, and her feeding him bacon he wouldn't take, so she ate it herself, and then she fixed some magic and fell asleep with Charlie, made out of sticks and rags and pebbles, but still warm and her very own son, slumbering and nice in her shaking mother arms . . . and they talked about golden things in drowsy voices until dawn made the fire slowly, slowly wither out . . .

4. Flight

Doris Lessing

Above the old man's head was the dovecote, a tall wire-netted shelf on stilts, full of strutting, preening birds. The sunlight broke on their grey breasts into small rainbows. His ears were lulled by their crooning, his hands stretched up towards his favourite, a homing pigeon, a young plump-bodied bird which stood still when it saw him and cocked a shrewd bright eye.

'Pretty, pretty, pretty,' he said, as he grasped the bird and drew it down, feeling the cold coral claws tighten around his finger. Content, he rested the bird lightly on his chest, and leaned against a tree, gazing out beyond the dovecote into the landscape of a late afternoon. In folds and hollows of sunlight and shade, the dark red soil, which was broken into great dusty clods, stretched wide to a tall horizon. Trees marked the course of the valley; a stream of rich green grass the road.

His eyes travelled homewards along this road until he saw his grand-daughter swinging on the gate underneath a frangipani* tree. Her hair fell down her back in a wave of sunlight, and her long bare legs repeated the angles of the frangipani stems, bare, shining-brown stems among patterns of pale blossoms.

She was gazing past the pink flowers, past the railway cottage where they lived, along the road to the village.

His mood shifted. He deliberately held out his wrist for the bird to take flight, and caught it again at the moment it spread its wings. He felt the plump shape strive and strain under his fingers; and, in a sudden access of troubled spite, shut the bird into a small box and fastened the bolt. 'Now you stay there,' he muttered; and turned his back on the shelf of birds. He moved warily along the hedge, stalking his grand-daughter, who was now looped over the gate, her head loose on her arms, singing. The light happy sound mingled with the crooning of the birds, and his anger mounted.

---

* Red jasmine tree.

'Hey!' he shouted; saw her jump, look back, and abandon the gate. Her eyes veiled themselves, and she said in a pert neutral voice: 'Hullo, Grandad.' Politely she moved towards him, after a lingering backward glance at the road.

'Waiting for Steven, hey?' he said, his fingers curling like claws into his palm.

'Any objection?' she asked lightly, refusing to look at him.

He confronted her, his eyes narrowed, shoulders hunched, tight in a hard knot of pain which included the preening birds, the sunlight, the flowers, herself. He said: 'Think you're old enough to go courting, hey?'

The girl tossed her head at the old-fashioned phrase and sulked, 'Oh, Grandad!'

'Think you want to leave home, hey? Think you can go running around the fields at night?'

Her smile made him see her, as he had every evening of this warm end-of-summer month, swinging hand in hand along the road to the village with that red-handed, red-throated, violent-bodied youth, the son of the postmaster. Misery went to his head and he shouted angrily: 'I'll tell your mother!'

'Tell away!' she said, laughing, and went back to the gate.

He heard her singing, for him to hear:

>'I've got you under my skin,
>I've got you deep in the heart of . . .'

'Rubbish,' he shouted. 'Rubbish. Impudent little bit of rubbish'

Growling under his breath he turned towards the dovecote, which was his refuge from the house he shared with his daughter and her husband and their children. But now the house would be empty. Gone all the young girls with their laughter and their squabbling and their teasing. He would be left, uncherished and alone, with that square-fronted, calm-eyed woman, his daughter.

He stooped, muttering, before the dovecote, resenting the absorbed cooing birds.

From the gate the girl shouted: 'Go and tell! Go on, what are you waiting for?'

Obstinately he made his way to the house, with quick,

pathetic, persistent glances of appeal back at her. But she never looked around. Her defiant but anxious young body stung him into love and repentance. He stopped. 'But I never meant . . .' he muttered, waiting for her to turn and run to him. 'I didn't mean . . .'

She did not turn. She had forgotten him. Along the road came the young man Steven, with something in his hand. A present for her? The old man stiffened as he watched the gate swing back, and the couple embrace. In the brittle shadows of the frangipani tree his grand-daughter, his darling, lay in the arms of the postmaster's son, and her hair flowed back over his shoulder.

'I see you!' shouted the old man spitefully. They did not move. He stumped into the little white-washed house, hearing the wooden veranda creak angrily under his feet. His daughter was sewing in the front room, threading a needle held to the light.

He stopped again, looking back into the garden. The couple were now sauntering among the bushes, laughing. As he watched he saw the girl escape from the youth with a sudden mischievous movement, and run off through the flowers with him in pursuit. He heard shouts, laughter, a scream, silence.

'But it's not like that at all,' he muttered miserably. 'It's not like that. Why can't you see? Running and giggling, and kissing and kissing. You'll come to something quite different.'

He looked at his daughter with sardonic hatred, hating himself. They were caught and finished, both of them, but the girl was still running free.

'Can't you *see?*' he demanded of his invisible grand-daughter, who was at that moment lying in the thick green grass with the postmaster's son.

His daughter looked at him and her eyebrows went up in tired forbearance.

'Put your birds to bed?' she asked, humouring him.

'Lucy,' he said urgently. 'Lucy . . .'

'Well what is it now?'

'She's in the garden with Steven.'

'Now you just sit down and have your tea.'

He stumped his feet alternately, thump, thump, on the hollow wooden floor and shouted: 'She'll marry him. I'm telling you, she'll be marrying him next!'

His daughter rose swiftly, brought him a cup, set him a plate.

'I don't want any tea. I don't want it, I tell you.'

'Now, now,' she crooned. 'What's wrong with it? Why not?'

'She's eighteen. Eighteen!'

'I was married at seventeen and I never regretted it.'

'Liar,' he said. 'Liar. Then you should regret it. Why do you make your girls marry? It's you who do it. What do you do it for? Why?'

'The other three have done fine. They've three fine husbands. Why not Alice?'

'She's the last,' he mourned. 'Can't we keep her a bit longer?'

'Come, now, dad. She'll be down the road, that's all. She'll be here every day to see you.'

'But it's not the same.' He thought of the other three girls, transformed inside a few months from charming petulant spoiled children into serious young matrons.

'You never did like it when we married!' she said. 'Why not? Every time, it's the same. When I got married you made me feel like it was something wrong. And my girls the same. You get them all crying and miserable the way you go on. Leave Alice alone. She's happy.' She sighed, letting her eyes linger on the sunlit garden. 'She'll marry next month. There's no reason to wait.'

'You've said they can marry?' he said incredulously.

'Yes, dad, why not?' she said coldly, and took up her sewing.

His eyes stung, and he went out on to the veranda. Wet spread down over his chin and he took out a handkerchief and mopped his whole face. The garden was empty.

From around the corner came the young couple; but their faces were no longer set against him. On the wrist of the postmaster's son balanced a young pigeon, the light gleaming on its breast.

'For me?' said the old man, letting the drops shake off his chin. 'For me?'

'Do you like it?' The girl grabbed his hand and swung on it. 'It's for you, grandad. Steven brought it for you.' They hung about him, affectionate, concerned, trying to charm away his wet eyes and his misery. They took his arms and directed him to the shelf of birds, one on each side, enclosing him, petting him, saying wordlessly that nothing would be changed, nothing could change, and that they would be with him always. The bird was proof of it, they said, from their lying happy eyes, as they thrust it on him. 'There, grandad, it's yours. It's for you.'

They watched him as he held it on his wrist, stroking its soft, sunwarmed back, watching the wings lift and balance.

'You must shut it up for a bit,' said the girl intimately. 'Until it knows this is its home.'

'Teach your grandmother to suck eggs,' growled the old man.

Released by his half-deliberate anger, they fell back, laughing at him. 'We're glad you like it.' They moved off, now serious and full of purpose, to the gate, where they hung, backs to him, talking quietly. More than anything could, their grown-up seriousness shut him out, making him alone; also, it quietened him, took the sting out of their tumbling like puppies on the grass. They had forgotten him again. Well, so they should, the old man reassured himself, feeling his throat clotted with tears, his lips trembling. He held the new bird to his face, for the caress of its silken feathers. Then he shut it in a box and took out his favourite.

'*Now* you can go,' he said aloud. He held it poised, ready for flight while he looked down the garden towards the boy and the girl. Then, clenched in the pain of loss, he lifted the bird on his wrist and watched it soar. A whirr and a spatter of wings, and a cloud of birds rose into the evening from the dovecote.

At the gate Alice and Steven forgot their talk and watched the birds.

On the veranda, that woman, his daughter, stood gazing, her eyes shaded with a hand that still held her sewing.

It seemed to the old man that the whole afternoon had stilled to watch his gesture of self-command, that even the leaves of the trees had stopped shaking.

Dry-eyed and calm, he let his hands fall to his sides and stood erect, staring up into the sky.

The cloud of shining silver birds flew up and up, with a shrill cleaving of wings, over the dark ploughed land and the darker belts of trees, and the bright folds of grass, until they floated high in the sunlight, like a cloud of motes of dust.

They wheeled in a wide circle, tilting their wings so there was flash after flash of light, and one after another they dropped from the sunshine of the upper sky to shadow, one after another, returning to the shadowed earth over trees and grass and field, returning to the valley and the shelter of night.

The garden was all a fluster and a flurry of returning birds. Then silence, and the sky was empty.

The old man turned, slowly, taking his time; he lifted his eyes to smile proudly down the garden at his grand-daughter. She was staring at him. She did not smile. She was wide-eyed, and pale in the cold shadow, and he saw the tears run shivering off her face.

5. No Witchcraft for Sale

Doris Lessing

The Farquars had been childless for years when little Teddy was born; and they were touched by the pleasure of their servants, who brought presents of fowls and eggs and flowers to the homestead when they came to rejoice over the baby, exclaiming with delight over his downy golden head and his blue eyes. They congratulated Mrs Farquar as if she had achieved a very great thing, and she felt that she had – her smile for the lingering, admiring natives was warm and grateful.

Later, when Teddy had his first haircut, Gideon the cook picked up the soft gold tufts from the ground, and held them reverently in his hand. Then he smiled at the little boy and said: 'Little Yellow Head.' That became the native name for the child. Gideon and Teddy were great friends from the first. When Gideon had finished his work, he would lift Teddy on his shoulders to the shade of a big tree, and play with him there, forming curious little toys from twigs and leaves and grass, or shaping animals from wetted soil. When Teddy learned to walk it was often Gideon who crouched before him, clucking encouragement, finally catching him when he fell, tossing him up in the air till they both became breathless with laughter. Mrs Farquar was fond of the old cook because of his love for the child.

There was no second baby; and one day Gideon said: 'Ah missus, missus, the Lord above sent this one; Little Yellow Head is the most good thing we have in our house.' Because of that 'we' Mrs Farquar felt a warm impulse towards her cook; and at the end of the month she raised his wages. He had been with her now for several years; he was one of the few natives who had his wife and children in the compound and never wanted to go home to his kraal, which was some hundreds of miles away. Sometimes a small piccanin who had been born the same time as Teddy, could be seen peering from the edge of the bush, staring in awe at the little white boy with his miraculous fair hair and nothern blue eyes. The two little children would gaze at each other with a wide, interested gaze, and once Teddy put out his hand curiously to touch the black child's cheek and hair.

Gideon, who was watching, shook his head wonderingly, and said: 'Ah, missus, these are both children, and one will grow up to be a Baas, and one will be a servant'; and Mrs Farquar smiled and said sadly, 'Yes, Gideon, I was thinking the same.' She sighed. 'It is God's will,' said Gideon, who was a mission boy. The Farquars were very religious people; and this shared feeling about God bound servant and masters even closer together.

Teddy was about six years old when he was given a scooter, and discovered the intoxications of speed. All day he would fly around the homestead, in and out of flowerbeds, scattering squawking chickens and irritated dogs, finishing with a wide dizzying arc into the kitchen door. There he would cry 'Gideon, look at me!' And Gideon would laugh and say: 'Very clever, Little Yellow Head.' Gideon's youngest son, who was now a herdsboy, came especially up from the compound to see the scooter. He was afraid to come near it, but Teddy showed off in front of him. 'Piccanin,' shouted Teddy, 'get out of my way!' And he raced in circles around the black child until he was frightened, and fled back to the bush.

'Why did you frighten him?' asked Gideon, gravely reproachful.

Teddy said defiantly: 'He's only a black boy,' and laughed. Then, when Gideon turned away from him without speaking, his face fell. Very soon he slipped into the house and found an orange and brought it to Gideon, saying: 'This is for you.' He could not bring himself to say he was sorry; but he could not bear to lose Gideon's affection either. Gideon took the orange unwillingly and sighed. 'Soon you will be going away to school, Little Yellow Head,' he said wonderingly, 'and then you will be grown up.' He shook his head gently and said, 'And that is how our lives go.' He seemed to be putting a distance between himself and Teddy, not because of resentment, but in the way a person accepts something inevitable. The baby had lain in his arms and smiled up into his face: the tiny boy had swung from his shoulders, had played with him by the hour. Now Gideon would not let his flesh touch the flesh of the white child. He was kind, but there was a grave formality in his voice that made Teddy pout and sulk away. Also, it made him into a man: with Gideon he was polite, and carried himself formally, and if he came into the kitchen to ask for something, it was in the way a white man uses towards a servant, expecting to be obeyed.

But on the day that Teddy came staggering into the kitchen with his fists to his eyes, shrieking with pain, Gideon dropped the pot full of hot soup that he was holding, rushed to the child, and forced aside his fingers. 'A snake!' he exclaimed. Teddy had been on his scooter, and had come to a rest with his foot on the side of a big tub of plants. A tree-snake, hanging by its tail from the roof, had spat full into his eyes. Mrs Farquar came running when she heard the commotion. 'He'll go blind,' she sobbed, holding Teddy close against her. 'Gideon, he'll go blind!' Already the eyes, with perhaps half an hour's sight left in them, were swollen up to the size of fists: Teddy's small white face was distorted by great purple oozing protuberances. Gideon said: 'Wait a minute, missus, I'll get some medicine.' He ran off into the bush.

Mrs Farquar lifted the child into the house and bathed his eyes with permanganate. She had scarcely heard Gideon's words; but when she saw that her remedies had no effect at all, and remembered how she had seen natives with no sight in their eyes, because of the spitting of a snake, she began to look for the return of her cook, remembering what she had heard of the efficacy of native herbs. She stood by the window, holding the terrified, sobbing little boy in her arms, and peered helplessly into the bush. It was not more than a few minutes before she saw Gideon come bounding back, and in his hand he held a plant.

'Do not be afraid, missus,' said Gideon, 'this will cure Little Yellow Head's eyes.' He stripped the leaves from the plant, leaving a small white fleshy root. Without even washing it, he put the root in his mouth, chewed it vigorously, then held the spittle there while he took the child forcibly from Mrs Farquar. He gripped Teddy down between his knees, and pressed the balls of his thumbs into the swollen eyes, so that the child screamed and

Mrs Farquar cried out in protest: 'Gideon, Gideon!' But Gideon took no notice. He knelt over the writhing child, pushing back the puffy lids till chinks of eyeball showed, and then he spat hard, again and again, into first one eye, and then the other. He finally lifted Teddy gently into his mother's arms, and said: 'His eyes will get better.' But Mrs Farquar was weeping with terror, and she could hardly thank him: it was impossible to believe that Teddy could keep his sight. In a couple of hours the swellings were gone; the eyes were inflamed and tender but Teddy could see. Mr and Mrs Farquar went to Gideon in the kitchen and thanked him over and over again. They felt helpless because of their gratitude: it seemed they could do nothing to express it. They gave Gideon presents for his wife and children, and a big increase in wages, but these things could not pay for Teddy's now completely cured eyes. Mrs Farquar said: 'Gideon, God chose you as an instrument for His goodness,' and Gideon said: 'Yes, missus, God is very good.'

Now, when such a thing happens on a farm, it cannot be long before everyone hears of it. Mr and Mrs Farquar told their neighbours and the story was discussed from one end of the district to the other. The bush is full of secrets. No one can live in Africa, or at least on the veld, without learning very soon that there is an ancient wisdom of leaf and soil and season – and, too, perhaps most important of all, of the darker tracts of the human mind – which is the black man's heritage. Up and down the district people were telling anecdotes, reminding each other of things that had happened to them.

'But I saw it myself, I tell you. It was a puff-adder bite. The kaffir's arm was swollen to the elbow, like a great shiny black bladder. He was groggy after half a minute. He was dying. Then suddenly a kaffir walked out of the bush with his hands full of green stuff. He smeared something on the place, and next day my boy was back at work, and all you could see was two small punctures in the skin.'

This was the kind of tale they told. And, as always, with a certain amount of exasperation, because while all of them knew that in the bush of Africa are waiting valuable drugs locked in bark, in simple-looking leaves, in roots, it was impossible to ever get the truth about them from the natives themselves.

The story eventually reached town; and perhaps it was at a sundowner party, or some such function, that a doctor, who happened to be there, challenged it. 'Nonsense,' he said. 'These things get exaggerated in the telling. We are always checking up on this kind of story, and we draw a blank every time.'

Anyway, one morning there arrived a strange car at the homestead, and out stepped one of the workers from the laboratory in town, with cases full of test-tubes and chemicals.

Mr and Mrs Farquar were flustered and pleased and flattered. They asked the scientist to lunch, and they told the story all over again, for the hundredth time. Little Teddy was there too, his blue eyes sparkling with health, to prove the truth of it. The scientist explained how humanity might benefit if this new drug could be offered for sale; and the Farquars were even more pleased: they were kind, simple people, who liked to think of something good coming about because of them. But when the scientist began talking of the money that might result, their manner showed discomfort. Their feelings over the miracle (that was how they thought of it) were so strong and deep and religious, that it was distasteful to them to think of money. The scientist, seeing their faces, went back to his first point, which was the advancement of humanity. He was perhaps a trifle perfunctory: it was not the first time he had come salting the tail of a fabulous bush-secret.

Eventually, when the meal was over, the Farquars called Gideon into their living-room and explained to him that this baas, here, was a Big Doctor from the Big City, and he had come all the way to see Gideon. At this Gideon seemed afraid; he did not understand; and Mrs Farquar explained quickly that it was because of the wonderful thing he had done with Teddy's eyes that the Big Baas had come.

Gideon looked from Mrs Farquar to Mr Farquar, and then at the little boy, who was showing great importance because of the occasion. At last he said grudgingly: 'The Big Baas wants to know what medicine I used?' He spoke incredulously, as if he could not believe his old friends could so betray him. Mr Farquar began explaining how a useful medicine could be made out of the root, and how it could be put on sale, and how thousands of people, black and white, up and down the continent of Africa, could be saved by the medicine when that spitting snake filled their eyes with poison. Gideon listened, his eyes bent on the ground, the skin of his forehead puckering in discomfort. When Mr Farquar had finished he did not reply. The scientist, who all this time had been leaning back in a big chair, sipping his coffee and smiling with sceptical good humour, chipped in and explained all over again, in different words, about the making of drugs and the progress of science. Also, he offered Gideon a present.

There was silence after this further explanation, and then Gideon remarked indifferently that he could not remember the root. His face was sullen and hostile, even when he looked at the Farquars, whom he usually treated like old friends. They were beginning to feel annoyed; and this feeling annulled the guilt that had been sprung into life by Gideon's accusing manner. They were beginning to feel that he was unreasonable. But it was at that moment that they all realized he would never give in. The magical drug would remain where it was, unknown and useless except for the tiny scattering of Africans who had the knowledge, natives who might be digging a ditch for the municipality in a ragged shirt and a pair of patched shorts, but who were still born to healing, hereditary healers, being the nephews or sons of the old witch doctors whose ugly masks and bits of bone and all the uncouth properties of magic were the outward signs of real power and wisdom.

The Farquars might tread on that plant fifty times a day as they passed from house to garden, from cow kraal to mealie field, but they would never know it.

But they went on persuading and arguing, with all the force of their exasperation; and Gideon continued to say that he could not remember, or that there was no such root, or that it was the wrong season of the year, or that it wasn't the root itself, but the spit from the mouth that had cured Teddy's eyes. He said all these things one after another, and seemed not to care they were contradictory. He was rude and stubborn. The Farquars could hardly recognize their gentle, lovable old servant in this ignorant, perversely obstinate African, standing there in front of them with lowered eyes, his hands twitching his cook's apron, repeating over and over whichever one of the stupid refusals that first entered his head.

And suddenly he appeared to give in. He lifted his head, gave a long, blank angry look at the circle of whites, who seemed to him like a circle of yelping dogs pressing around him, and said: 'I will show you the root.'

They walked single file away from the homestead down a kaffir path. It was a blazing December afternoon, with the sky full of hot rain-clouds. Everything was hot: the sun was like a bronze tray whirling overhead, there was a heat shimmer over the fields, the soil was scorching underfoot, the dusty wind blew gritty and thick and warm in their faces. It was a terrible day, fit only for reclining on a veranda with iced drinks, which is where they would normally have been at that hour.

From time to time, remembering that on the day of the snake it had taken ten minutes to find the root, someone asked: 'Is it much farther, Gideon?' And Gideon would answer over his shoulder, with angry politeness: 'I'm looking for the root, baas.' And indeed, he would frequently bend sideways and trail his hand among the grasses with a gesture that was insulting in its perfunctoriness. He walked them through the bush along unknown paths for two hours, in that melting destroying heat, so that the sweat trickled coldly down them and their heads ached. They were all quite silent: the Farquars because they were angry, the scientist because he was being proved right again; there was no such plant. His was a tactful silence.

At last, six miles from the house, Gideon suddenly decided they had had enough; or perhaps his anger evaporated at that moment. He picked up, without an attempt at looking anything but casual, a handful of blue flowers from the grass, flowers that had been growing plentifully all down the paths they had come.

He handed them to the scientist without looking at him, and marched of by himself on the way home, leaving them to follow him if they chose.

When they got back to the house, the scientist went to the kitchen to thank Gideon: he was being very polite, even though there was an amused look in his eyes. Gideon was not there. Throwing the flowers casually into the back of his car, the eminent visitor departed on his way back to his laboratory.

Gideon was back in his kitchen in time to prepare dinner, but he was sulking. He spoke to Mrs Farquar like an unwilling servant. It was days before they liked each other again.

The Farquars made enquiries about the root from their labourers. Sometimes they were answered with distrustful stares. Sometimes the natives said: 'We do not know. We have never heard of the root.' One, the cattle boy, who had been with them a long time, and had grown to trust them a little, said: 'Ask your boy in the kitchen. Now, there's a doctor for you. He's the son of a famous medicine man who used to be in these parts, and there's nothing he cannot cure.' Then he added politely: 'Of course, he's not as good as the white man's doctor, we know that, but he's good for us.'

After some time, when the soreness had gone from between the Farquars and Gideon, they began to joke: 'When are you going to show us the snake-root, Gideon?' And he would laugh and shake his head, saying, a little uncomfortably: 'But I did show you, missus, have you forgotten?'

Much later, Teddy, as a schoolboy, would come into the kitchen and say: 'You old rascal, Gideon! Do you remember that time you tricked us all by making us walk miles all over the veld for nothing? It was so far my father had to carry me!'

And Gideon would double up with polite laughter. After much laughing, he would suddenly straighten himself up, wipe his old eyes, and look sadly at Teddy, who was grinning mischievously at him across the kitchen: 'Ah, Little Yellow Head, how you have grown! Soon you will be grown up with a farm of your own . . .'

6. The Healing

Dorothy Nimmo

We were messing about, which we shouldn't have been doing, but there you are. We should have been outside, but it was freezing out. Karen was showing off doing this flip thing she's just learnt. I don't mind Karen showing off because she's been my friend since the Junior and she's really good, anyway. Then she sort of slipped and she just lay there on the floor.

'Oh Lord,' she said. 'That's torn it!'

And we remembered about the competition.

You might think we were making a big thing about it but there wasn't much you could do around our school that made people think anything of you. Everyone wants to be someone, I mean everyone wants to be special. Don't they? Look at all the people who go on the prize shows on the telly, they'd rather look like prize wallies and be able to say they've been on the telly than spend their whole lives never doing anything.

At our school you do all right if you play football. If you get in the team you do all right. And the big boys have their bikes. They start with the mopeds and then they get the big Hondas, with the fairings and that. They're really big deal on those bikes, with their leathers and boots and their heads twice the proper size in the helmets. You can't see the spots under the visors. And the girls hang round them. There isn't much for the girls. You get noticed if you go around, you know, if you're easy, and if you get pregnant they talk about you but they don't admire you. There isn't much a girl can do apart from swimming and gymnastics.

They put us all in for the competitions, that's the way they have. They think there's no point in anything unless there's a competition and a prize. They mean well, they think we're losers so they'll give us a chance at something, even if it's something really diddy, like cookery. They had a cookery competition one time, it was some custard-powder company, they all had to think up different things you could make with custard powder. Sandra went in for that because there was a prize, twenty pounds. She made this cake with custard powder and then custard on top, you know, and then all different fruit; it was a lovely colour, really bright yellow, but she didn't win. My Mum does flower arrangements. Honestly, she spends hours finding this stuff, dried flowers and leaves, and she has all these different baskets and bits of log hollowed out. I think it looks terrible. It looks dead and it stands around the house all winter getting deader and deader. But she puts these things in the Flower Show and gets prizes; she gets a real kick out of the prizes. So she says to me, 'Why don't you make a sponge cake, Marty, there's a class here for a sponge? Or scones, that's easy, go on. Just for fun. It doesn't matter if you win or not, that's not the point. It's the competition is the fun!'

I don't understand her. What's the point of going in for it if you know you're going to lose? It isn't fun, it's bloody murder, I think.

Karen used to go in for swimming. She said it was boring pounding up and down the pool. When they get keen they really drive you. It must do something for them, I suppose it would, for the teachers, if they can get a winner out of all of us losers. Karen was good at the swimming, but then she got something wrong with her ears and even old Evans thought it was a bit much to go deaf just so the school could get into the area championships. So then she took up the gymnastics.

Ever since I've known her she's been doing things like the crab, going round the playground all bent over backwards, and cartwheels and that, so she'd got the talent and she really took to it. Everyone was doing it that year, it was all on the telly and the girls were really keen, but it was Karen they kept on at to do the competitions. And there was Karen on the floor. The Championship was the next day.

Someone said she ought to go to the nurse and someone else said, try a hot-water bottle. Sandra said, 'What about an iron?' And we said, 'What do you mean, an iron?'

'You iron her back,' said Sandra, 'I've seen it done.'

'You're having me on,' I said.

'It's the heat,' said Sandra.

'Honestly?' said Pam. Pam believes anything, always has. One time I told her if she put her fingers down her throat she could touch her toes. She believed me. She was sick, you can imagine, all on her shoes.

'What about a rolling pin?' I said, 'we could roll her out.' I didn't think they'd take that seriously.

'I think we ought to go and tell Mr Evans,' said Jenny.

'How are you feeling?' I asked Karen.

'Not bad,' she said. So I knew she felt bad.

'We'd better sort it out for ourselves if we can,' I said.

So then Sandra went and got in at the window on the Home Economics, which is easy for her. I reckon she can get into anything, it's a knack, she says. It'll get her into trouble. She got in at the window and then she got another window open and we all climbed in. Karen said it was easing up a bit, but we made her lie down on one of the tables. First we found the rolling pin and rolled it up and down. You wouldn't think that would do any good; it didn't.

'Roll on a floured board,' said Nell. 'That's what it says in the cookery books!' She thought that was such a good joke she was no help at all for a bit.

'Is that what it means?' said Pam, 'Honestly?'

'Oh Pam!' said Sandra.

Then we got out the iron, Sandra got the cupboard open, and we plugged it in and started ironing Karen's back through her vest until it got too hot and she yelled. And we'd had it on the lowest setting.

Then it was Nell said, 'Let's try the laying-on of hands.'

'Go on,' said Karen, 'what's that?'

'It's what Jesus did, what the healing people do, you know, like in the Bible.'

'I never get in in time for Assembly,' I said.

'We don't have Bible in Assembly any more,' said Pam.

'We always have sex in RE,' said Jenny.

'But we had it in the Junior,' said Nell, 'Jesus was always at it, putting his hands on people. And they do it up at the Pentecostal. There's a man used to come to the shop ever so lame and now he doesn't.'

'Go on Karen, let's have a go,' said Sandra.

'Do you have to say anything?'

'Pick up your bed and walk,' suggested Nell.

I'm not on my bed,' said Karen.

'In the name of the Father and the Son and the Holy Ghost, amen?'

'I don't know,' said Sandra. 'You go first.'

Nell put her hands on Karen's back and said, 'Get thee behind me, Satan!'

I don't know where she got that from.

Nothing happened. We didn't expect anything to happen, we were just trying it on. Then Pam put her hands on and began stroking and squeezing like the massage people do in the films, but Karen said that made it worse. And then I did it. I put my hands on Karen's back and I could feel the warmth going on down my arm and running into her back. I felt like it was my blood running into her and if I didn't take my hands away I wouldn't have any blood left any more. It was quite hard, taking my hands away. I felt quite weak, honestly.

Karen lay there for a bit. Then she got up.

'How does it feel?' I said.

'It's fine,' she said. 'That's fixed it.'

Then they all started to go on at me.

'What did you do, Mart?' said Sandra.

'I didn't do anything.'

'You must have done something.'

'Try it on me,' said Nell.

'I've got this dirty great spot on my chin,' said Sandra.

'I've got warts,' said Jenny.

But Karen said to leave me alone, we'd better get out before someone caught us.

Karen was third in the competition. Mr Evans said it wasn't good enough.

Sometimes Nell or Sandra get at me about it. If they have a headache or a period pain they say, 'What about a bit of the old laying-on of hands, Mart?' But I don't take any notice. They'll forget about it.

I wouldn't like to do it again.

They probably have competitions for that, too. If they knew about it, they'd probably put me in for them. I can just imagine all the sick, lame people laid out on the floor and everyone having a go who can make them get up fastest. With stopwatches and numbers, like they do in competitions. And prizes. I know they don't really. I don't expect I'd win if they did.

7. Revenge

Ellen Gilchrist

It was the summer of the Broad Jump Pit.

The Broad Jump Pit, how shall I describe it! It was a bright orange rectangle in the middle of a green pasture. It was three feet deep, filled with river sand and sawdust. A real cinder tack led up to it, ending where tall poles for pole-vaulting rose forever in the still Delta air.

I am looking through the old binoculars. I am watching Bunky coming at a run down the cinder path, pausing expertly at the jump-off line, then rising into the air, heels stretched far out in front of him, landing in the sawdust. Before the dust has settled Saint John comes running with the tape, calling out measurements in his high, excitable voice.

Next comes my thirteen-year-old brother, Dudley, coming at a brisk jog down the track, the pole-vaulting pole held lightly in his delicate hands, then vaulting, high into the sky. His skinny tanned legs make a last, desperate surge, and he is clear and over.

Think how it looked from my lonely exile atop the chicken house. I was ten years old, the only girl in a house full of cousins. There were six of us, shipped to the Delta for the summer, dumped on my grandmother right in the middle of a world war.

They built this wonder in answer to a V-Mail letter from my father in Europe. The war was going well, my father wrote, within a year the Allies would triumph over the forces of evil, the world would be at peace, and the Olympic torch would again be brought down from its mountain and carried to Zurich or Amsterdam or London or Mexico City, wherever free men lived and worshipped sports. My father had been a participant in any Olympic even when he was young.

Therefore, the letter continued, Dudley and Bunky and Philip and Saint John and Oliver were to begin training. The United States would need athletes now, not soldiers.

They were to train for broad jumping and pole-vaulting and discus throwing, for fifty-, one-hundred-, and four-hundred-yard dashes, for high and low hurdles. The letter included instructions for building the pit, for making pole-vaulting poles out of cane, and for converting ordinary sawhorses into hurdles. It ended with a page of tips for proper eating and admonished Dudley to take good care of me as I was my father's own dear sweet little girl.

The letter came one afternoon. Early the next morning they began construction. Around noon I wandered out to the pasture to see how they were coming along. I picked up a shovel.

'Put that down, Rhoda,' Dudley said. 'Don't bother us now. We're working.'

'I know it,' I said. 'I'm going to help.'

'No, you're not,' Bunky said. 'This is the Broad Jump Pit. We're starting our training.'

'I'm going to do it too,' I said. 'I'm going to be in training.'

'Get out of here now,' Dudley said. 'This is only for boys, Rhoda. This isn't a game.'

'I'm going to dig it if I want to,' I said, picking up a shovelful of dirt and throwing it on Philip. On second thought I picked up another shovelful and threw it on Bunky.

'Get out of here, Ratface,' Philip yelled at me. 'You German spy.' He was referring to the initials on my Girl Scout uniform.

'You goddamn niggers,' I yelled. 'You niggers. I'm digging this if I want to and you can't stop me, you nasty niggers, you Japs, you Jews.' I was throwing dirt on everyone now. Dudley grabbed the shovel and wrestled me to the ground. He held my arms down in the coarse grass and peered into my face.

'Rhoda, you're not having anything to do with this Broad Jump Pit. And if you set foot inside this pasture or come around here and touch anything we will break your legs and drown you in the bayou with a crowbar around your neck.' He was twisting my leg until it creaked at the joints. 'Do you get it, Rhoda? Do you understand me?'

'Let me up,' I was screaming, my rage threatening to split open my skull. 'Let me up, you goddamn nigger, you Jap, you spy. I'm telling Grannie and you're going to get the worst whipping of your life. And you better quit digging this hole for the horses to fall in. Let me up, let me up. Let me go.'

'You've been ruining everything we've thought up all summer,' Dudley said, 'And you're not setting foot inside this pasture.'

In the end they dragged me back to the house, and I ran screaming into the kitchen where Grannie and Calvin, the black man who did the cooking, tried to comfort me, feeding me pound cake and offering to let me help with the mayonnaise.

'You be a sweet girl, Rhoda,' my grandmother said, 'and this afternoon we'll go over to Eisenglas Plantation to play with Miss Ann Wentzel.'

'I don't want to play with Miss Ann Wentzel,' I screamed. 'I hate Miss Ann Wentzel. She's fat and she calls me a Yankee. She said my socks were ugly.'

'Why, Rhoda,' my grandmother said. 'I'm surprised at you. Miss Ann Wentzel is your own sweet friend. Her momma was your momma's roommate at All Saints'. How can you talk like that?'

'She's a nigger,' I screamed. 'She's a goddamned nigger German spy.'

'Now it's coming. Here comes the temper,' Calvin said, rolling his eyes back in their sockets to make me madder. I threw my second fit in the morning, beating my fists into a door frame. My grandmother seized me in soft arms. She led me to a bedroom where I sobbed myself to sleep in a sea of down pillows.

The construction went on for several weeks. As soon as they finished breakfast every morning they started out for the pasture. Wood had to be burned to make cinders, sawdust brought from the sawmill, sand hauled up from the riverbank by wheelbarrow.

When the pit was finished the savage training began. From my several vantage points I watched them. Up and down, up and down they ran, dove, flew, sprinted. Drenched with sweat they wrestled each other to the ground in bitter feuds over distances and times and fractions of inches.

Dudley was their self-appointed leader. He drove them like a demon. They began each morning by running around the edge of the pasture several times, then practising their hurdles and dashes, then on to discus throwing and callisthenics. Then on to the Broad Jump Pit with its endless challenges.

They even pressed the old mare into service. Saint John was from New Orleans and knew the British ambassador and was thinking of being a polo player. Up and down the pasture he drove the poor old creature, leaning far out of the saddle, swatting a basketball with my grandaddy's cane.

I spied on them from the swing that went out over the bayou, and from the roof the chicken house, and sometimes from the pasture fence itself, calling out insults or attempts to make them jealous.

'Guess what,' I would yell, 'I'm going to town to the Chinaman's store.' 'Guess what, I'm getting to go to the beauty parlour.' 'Doctor Biggs says you're adopted.'

They ignored me. At meals they sat together at one end of the table, making jokes about my temper and my red hair, opening their mouths so I could see their half-chewed food, burping loudly in my direction.

At night they pulled their cots together on the sleeping porch, plotting against me while I slept beneath my grandmother's window, listening to the soft assurance of her snoring.

I began to pray the Japs would win the war, would come marching into Issaquena County and take them prisoners, starving and torturing them, sticking bamboo splinters under their fingernails. I saw myself in the Japanese colonel's office, turning them in, writing their names down, myself being treated like an honoured guest, drinking tea from tiny blue cups like the ones the Chinaman had in his store.

They would be outside, tied up with wire. There would be Dudley, begging for mercy. What good to him now his loyal gang, his photographic memory, his trick magnet dogs, his perfect pitch, his camp shorts, his Baby Brownie camera.

I prayed they would get polio, would be consigned forever to iron lungs. I put myself to sleep at night imagining their laboured breathing, their five little wheelchairs lined up by the store as I drove by in my father's Packard, my arm around the jacket of his blue uniform, on my way to Hollywood for my screen test.

Meanwhile, I practised dancing. My grandmother had a black housekeeper named Baby Doll who was a wonderful dancer. In the mornings I followed her around while she dusted, begging for dancing lessons. She was a big woman, as tall as a man, and gave off a dark rich smell, an unforgettable incense, a combination of Evening in Paris and the sweet perfume of the cabins.

Baby Doll wore bright skirts and on her blouses a pin that said REMEMBER, then a real pearl, then HARBOR. She was engaged to a sailor and was going to California to be rich as soon as the war was over.

I would put a stack of heavy, scratched records on the record player, and Baby Doll and I would dance through the parlours to the music of Glenn Miller or Guy Lombardo or Tommy Dorsey.

Sometimes I stood on a stool in front of the fire-place and made up lyrics while Baby Doll acted them out, moving lightly across the old dark rugs, turning and swooping and shaking and gliding.

Outside the summer sun beat down on the Delta, beating down a million volts a minute, feeding the soybeans and cotton and clover, sucking Steele's Bayou up into the clouds, beating down on the road and the store, on the pecans and elms and magnolias, on the men at work in the fields, on the athletes at work in the pasture.

Inside Baby Doll and I would be dancing. Or Guy Lombardo would be playing 'Begin the Beguine' and I would be belting out lyrics.

> 'Oh, let them begin . . . we don't care,
> America all . . . ways does it share
> We'll be there with plenty of ammo,
> Allies . . . don't ever despair . . .'

Baby Doll thought I was a genius. If I was having an especially creative morning she would go running

out to the kitchen and bring anyone she could find
to hear me.

'Oh, let them begin any warrr . . .' I would be singing,
tapping one foot against the fire-place tiles, waving my
arms around like a conductor.

> 'Uncle Sam will fight
> for the underrr . . . doggg.
> Never fear, Allies, never fear.'

A new record would drop. Baby Doll would swoop
me into her fragrant arms, and we would break into an
improvisation on Tommy Dorsey's 'Boogie-Woogie.'

But the Broad Jump Pit would not go away. It
loomed in my dreams. If I walked to the store I
had to pass the pasture. If I stood on the porch or
looked out my grandmother's window, there it was,
shimmering in the sunlight, constantly guarded by one of
the Olympians.

Things went from bad to worse between me and
Dudley. If we so much as passed each other in the hall a
fight began. He would hold up his fists and dance around,
trying to look like a fighter. When I came flailing at him
he would reach underneath my arms and punch me in
the stomach.

I considered poisoning him. There was a box of white
powder in the toolshed with a skull and crossbones
above the label. Several times I took it down and
held it in my hands, shuddering at the power it gave
me. Only the thought of the electric chair kept me
from using it.

Every day Dudley gathered his troops and headed out
for the pasture. Every day my hatred grew and festered.
Then, just about the time I could stand it no longer, a
diversion occurred.

One afternoon about four o'clock an official-looking
sedan clattered across the bridge and came roaring down
the road to the house.

It was my cousin, Lauralee Manning, wearing her
WAVE uniform and smoking Camels in an ivory holder.
Lauralee had been widowed at the beginning of the war
when her young husband crashed his Navy training plane
into the Pacific.

Lauralee dried her tears, joined the WAVES, and went off to avenge his death. I had not seen this paragon since I was a small child, bu I had memorized the photograph Miss Onnie Maud, who was Lauralee's mother, kept on her dresser. It was a photograph of Lauralee leaning against the rail of a destroyer.

Not that Lauralee ever went to sea on a destroyer. She was spending the war in Pensacola, Florida, being secretary to an admiral.

Now, out of a clear blue sky, here was Lauralee, home on leave with a two-carat diamond ring and the news that she was getting married.

'You might have called and given some warning,' Miss Onnie Maud said, turning Lauralee into a mass of wrinkles with her embraces. 'You could have softened the blow with a letter.'

'Who's the groom?' my grandmother said. 'I only hope he's not a pilot.'

'Is he an admiral?' I said, 'or a colonel or a major or a commander?'

'My fiancé's not in uniform, honey,' Lauralee said. 'He's in real estate. He runs the war-bond effort for the whole state of Florida. Last year he collected half a million dollars.'

'In real estate!' Miss Onnie Maud said, gasping. 'What religion is he?'

'He's Unitarian,' she said. 'His name is Donald Marcus. He's best friends with Admiral Semmes, that's how I met him. And he's coming a week from Saturday, and that's all the time we have to get ready for the wedding.'

'Unitarian!' Miss Onnie Maud said. 'I don't think I've ever met a Unitarian.'

'Why isn't he in uniform?' I insisted.

'He has flat feet,' Lauralee said gaily. 'But you'll love him when you see him.'

Later that afternoon Lauralee took me off by myself for a ride in the sedan.

'Your mother is my favourite cousin,' she said, touching my face with gentle fingers. 'You'll look just like her when you grow up and get your figure.'

I moved closer, admiring the brass buttons on her starched uniform and the brisk way she shifted and braked and put in the clutch and accelerated.

We drove down the river road and out to the bootlegger's shack where Lauralee bought a pint of Jack Daniel's and two Cokes. She poured out half of her Coke, filled it with whiskey, and we roared off down the road with the radio playing.

We drove along in the lengthening day. Lauralee was chain-smoking, lighting one Camel after another, tossing the butts out the window, taking sips from her bourbon and Coke. I sat beside her, pretending to smoke a piece of rolled-up paper, making little noises into the mouth of my Coke bottle.

We drove up to a picnic spot on the levee and sat under a tree to look out at the river.

'I miss this old river,' she said. 'When I'm said I dream about it licking the tops of the levees.'

I didn't know what to say to that. To tell the truth I was afraid to say much of anything to Lauralee. She seemed so splendid. It was enough to be allowed to sit by her on the levee.

'Now, Rhoda,' she said, 'your mother was matron of honour in my wedding to Buddy, and I want you, her own little daughter, to be maid of honour in my second wedding.'

I could hardly believe my ears! While I was trying to think of something to say to this wonderful news I saw that Lauralee was crying, great tears were forming in her blue eyes.

'Under this very tree is where Buddy and I got engaged,' she said. Now the tears were really starting to roll, falling all over the front of her uniform. 'He gave me my ring right where we're sitting.'

'The maid of honour?' I said, patting her on the shoulder, trying to be of some comfort. 'You really mean the maid of honour?'

'Now he's gone from the world,' she continued, 'and I'm marrying a wonderful man, but that doesn't make it any easier. Oh, Rhoda, they never even found his body, never even found his body.'

I was patting her on the head now, afraid she would forget her offer in the midst of her sorrow.

'You mean I get to be the real maid of honour?'

'Oh, yes, Rhoda, honey,' she said. 'The maid of honour, my only attendant.' She blew her nose on a lace-trimmed handkerchief and sat up straighter, taking a drink from the Coke bottle.

'Not only that, but I have decided to let you pick out your own dress. We'll go to Greenville and you can try on every dress at Nell's and Blum's and you can have the one you like the most.'

I threw my arms around her, burning her with happiness, smelling her whiskey and Camels and the dark Tabu perfume that was her signature. Over her shoulder and through the low branches of the trees the afternoon sun was going down in an orgy of reds and blues and purples and violets, falling from sight, going all the way to china.

Let them keep their nasty Broad Jump Pit, I thought. Wait till they hear about this. Wait till they find out I'm maid of honour in a military wedding.

Finding the dress was another matter. Early the next morning Miss Onnie Maud and my grandmother and Lauralee and I set out for Greenville.

As we passed the pasture I hung out the back window making faces at the athletes. This time they only pretended to ignore me. They couldn't ignore this wedding. It was going to be in the parlour instead of the church so they wouldn't even get to be altar boys. They wouldn't get to light a candle.

'I don't know why you care what's going on in that pasture,' my grandmother said. 'Even if they let you play with them, all it would do is make you a lot of ugly muscles.'

'Then you'd have big old ugly arms like Weegie Toler,' Miss Onnie Maud said. 'Lauralee, you remember Weegie Toler, that was a swimmer. Her arms got so big no one would take her to a dance, much less marry her.'

'Well, I don't want to get married anyway,' I said. 'I'm never getting married. I'm going to New York City and be a lawyer.'

'Where does she get those ideas?' Miss Onnie Maud said.

'When you get older you'll want to get married,' Lauralee said. 'Look at how much fun you're having being in my wedding.'

'Well, I'm never getting married,' I said. 'And I'm never having any children. I'm going to New York and be a lawyer and save people from the electric chair.'

'It's the movies,' Miss Onnie Maud said. 'They let her watch anything she likes in Indiana.'

We walked into Nell's and Blum's Department Store and took up the largest dressing-room. My grandmother and Miss Onnie Maud were seated on brocade chairs and every saleslady in the store came crowding around trying to get in on the wedding.

I refused to even consider the dresses they brought from the 'girls'' department.

'I told her she could wear whatever she wanted,' Lauralee said, 'and I'm keeping my promise.'

'Well, she's not wearing green satin or I'm not coming,' my grandmother said, indicating the dress I had found on a rack and was clutching against me.

'At least let her try it on,' Lauralee said. 'Let her see for herself.' She zipped me into the green satin. It came down to my ankles and fit around my midsection like a girdle, making my waist seem smaller than my stomach. I admired myself in the mirror. It was almost perfect. I looked exactly like a nightclub singer.

'This one's fine,' I said. 'This is the one I want.'

'It looks marvellous, Rhoda,' Lauralee said, 'but it's the wrong colour for the wedding. Remember I'm wearing blue.'

'I believe the child's colour-blind,' Miss Onnie Maud said. 'It runs in her father's family.'

'I am not colour-blind,' I said, reaching behind me and unzipping the dress. 'I have twenty-twenty vision.'

'Let her try on some more,' Lauralee said. 'Let her try on everything in the store.'

I proceeded to do just that, with the salesladies getting grumpier and grumpier. I tried on a gold gabardine dress with a rhinestone-studded cummerbund, I tried on a pink ballerina-length formal and a lavender voile tea dress and several silk suits. Somehow nothing looked right.

'Maybe we'll have to make her something,' my grandmother said.

'But there's no time,' Miss Onnie Maud said. 'Besides first we'd have to find out what she wants. Rhoda, please tell us what you're looking for.'

Their faces all turned to mine, waiting for an answer. But I didn't know the answer.

The dress I wanted was a secret. The dress I wanted was dark and tall and thin as a reed. There was a word for what I wanted, a word I had seen in magazines. But what was that word? I could not remember.

'I want something dark,' I said at last. 'Something dark and silky.'

'Wait right there,' the saleslady said. 'Wait just a minute.' Then, from out of a pre-war storage closet she brought a black-watch plaid recital dress with spaghetti strips and a white piqué jacket. It was made of taffeta and rustled when I touched it. There was a label sewn into the collar of the jacket. *Little Miss Sophisticate*, it said. *Sophisticate*, that was the word I was seeking.

I put on the dress and stood triumphant in a sea of ladies and dresses and hangers.

'This is the dress,' I said. 'This is the dress I'm wearing.'

'It's perfect,' Lauralee said. 'Start hemming it up. She'll be the prettiest maid of honour in the whole world.'

All the way home I held the box on my lap thinking about how I would look in the dress. Wait till they see me like this, I was thinking. Wait till they see what I really look like.

I fell in love with the groom. The moment I laid eyes on him I forgot he was flat-footed. He arrived bearing gifts of music and perfume and candy, a warm dark-skinned man with eyes the colour of walnuts.

He laughed out loud when he saw me, standing on the porch with my hands on my hips.

'This must be Rhoda,' he exclaimed, 'the famous red-haired maid of honour.' He came running up the steps, gave me a slow, exciting hug, and presented me with a whole album of Xavier Cugat records. I had never owned a record of my own, much less an album.

Before the evening was over I put on a red formal I found in a trunk and did a South American dance for him to Xavier Cugat's 'Poinciana'. He said he had never seen anything like it in his whole life.

The wedding itself was a disappointment. No one came but the immediate family and there was no aisle to march down and the only music was Onnie Maud playing 'Liebstraum'.

Dudley and Philip and Saint John and Oliver and Bunky were dressed in long pants and white shirts and ties. They had fresh military crew cuts and looked like a nest of new birds, huddled together on the blue velvet sofa, trying to keep their hands to themselves, trying to figure out how to act at a wedding.

The elderly Episcopal priest read out the ceremony in a gravelly smoker's voice, ruining all the good parts by coughing. He was in a bad mood because Lauralee and Mr Marcus hadn't found the time to come to him for marriage instruction.

Still, I got to hold the bride's flowers while he gave her the ring and stood so close to her during the ceremony I could hear her breathing.

The reception was better. People came from all over the Delta. There were tables with candles set up around the porches and sprays of greenery in every corner. There were gentlemen sweating in linen suits and the record player playing every minute. In the back hall Calvin had set up a real professional bar with tall, permanently frosted glasses and ice and mint and lemons and every kind of whiskey and liqueur in the world.

I stood in the receiving line getting compliments on my dress, then wandered around the rooms eating cake and letting people hug me. After a while I got bored with that and went out to the back hall and began to fix myself a drink at the bar.

I took one of the frosted glasses and began filling it from different bottles, tasting as I went along. I used plenty of crème de menthe and soon had something that tasted heavenly. I filled the glass with crushed ice, added three straws, and went out to sit on the back steps and cool off.

I was feeling wonderful. A full moon was caught like a kite in the pecan trees across the river. I sipped along on my drink. Then, without planning it, I did something I had never dreamed of doing. I left the porch alone at night. Usually I was in terror of the dark. My grandmother had told me that alligators come out of the bayou to eat children who wander alone at night.

I walked out across the yard, the huge moon giving so much light I almost cast a shadow. When I was nearly to the water's edge I turned and looked back toward the house. It shimmered in the moonlight like a jukebox alive in a meadow, seemed to pulsate with music and laughter and people, beautiful and foreign, not a part of me.

I looked out at the water, then down the road to the pasture. The Broad Jump Pit! There it was, perfect and unguarded. Why had I never thought of doing this before?

I began to run toward the road. I ran as fast as my Mary Jane pumps would allow me. I pulled my dress up around my waist and climbed the fence in one motion, dropping lightly down on the other side. I was sweating heavily, alone with the moon and my wonderful courage.

I knew exactly what to do first. I picked up the pole and hoisted it over my head. It felt solid and balanced and alive. I hoisted it up and down a few times as I had seen Dudley do, getting the feel of it.

Then I laid it ceremoniously down on the ground, reached behind me, and unhooked the plaid formal. I left it lying in a heap on the ground. There I stood, in my cotton underpants, ready to take up pole-vaulting.

I lifted the pole and carried it back to the end of the cinder path. I ran slowly down the path, stuck the pole in the wooden cup, and attempted throwing my body into the air, using it as a lever.

Something was wrong. It was more difficult than it appeared from a distance. I tried again. Nothing happened. I sat down with the pole across my legs to think things over.

Then I remembered something I had watched Dudley doing through the binoculars. He measured down from the end of the pole with his fingers spread wide. That was it, I had to hold it closer to the end.

I tried it again. The time the pole lifted me several feet off the ground. My body sailed across the grass in a neat arc and I landed on my toes. I was a natural!

I do not know how long I was out there, running up and down the cinder path, thrusting my body further and further through space, tossing myself into the pit like a mussel shell thrown across the bayou.

At last I decided I was ready for the real test. I had to vault over a cane barrier. I examined the pegs on the wooden poles and chose one that came up to my shoulder.

I put the barrier pole in place, spit over my left shoulder, and marched back to the end of the path. Suck up your guts, I told myself. It's only a pole. It won't get stuck in your stomach and tear out your insides. It won't kill you.

I stood at the end of the path eyeballing the barrier. Then, above the incessant racket of crickets, I heard my name being called. Rhoda . . . the voices were calling. Rhoda . . . Rhoda . . . Rhoda . . . Rhoda.

I turned toward the house and saw them coming. Mr Marcus and Dudley and Bunky and Calvin and Lauralee and what looked like half the wedding. They were climbing the fence, calling my name, and coming to get me. Rhoda . . . they called out. Where on earth have you been? What on earth are you doing?

I hoisted the pole up to my shoulders and began to run down the path, running into the light from the moon. I picked up speed, thrust the pole into the cup, and threw myself into the sky, into the still Delta night. I sailed up and was clear and over the barrier.

I let go of the pole and began my fall, which seemed to last a long, long time. It was like falling through clear water. I dropped into the sawdust and lay very still, waiting for them to reach me.

Sometimes I think whatever has happened since has been of no real interest to me.

8. The Conversion of the Jews

Philip Roth

'You're a real one for opening your mouth in the first place,' Itzie said. 'What do you open your mouth all the time for?'

'I didn't bring it up, Itz, I didn't,' Ozzie said.

'What do you care about Jesus Christ for anyway?'

'I didn't bring up Jesus Christ. He did. I didn't even know what he was talking about. Jesus is historical, he kept saying. Jesus is historical.' Ozzie mimicked the monumental voice of Rabbi Binder.

'Jesus was a person that lived like you and me,' Ozzie continued. 'That's what Binder said –'

'Yeah? . . . So what! What do I give two cents whether he lived or not. And what do you gotta open your mouth!' Itzie Lieberman favoured closed-mouthedness, especially when it came to Ozzie Freedman's questions. Mrs Freedman had to see Rabbi Binder twice before about Ozzie's questions and this Wednesday at four-thirty would be the third time. Itzie preferred to keep *his* mother in the kitchen; he settled for behind-the-back subtleties such as gestures, faces, snarls and other less delicate barnyard noises.

'He was a real person, Jesus, but he wasn't like God, and we don't believe he is God.' Slowly, Ozzie was explaining Rabbi Binder's position to Itzie, who had been absent from Hebrew School the previous afternoon.

'The Catholics,' Itzie said helpfully, 'they believe in Jesus Christ, that he's God.' Itzie Lieberman used 'the Catholics' in its broadest sense – to include the Protestants.

Ozzie received Itzie's remark with a tiny head bob, as though it were a footnote, and went on. 'His mother was Mary, and his father probably was Joseph,' Ozzie said. 'But the New Testament says his real father was God.'

'His *real* father?'

'Yeah,' Ozzie said, 'that's the big thing, his father's supposed to be God.'

'Bull.'

'That's what Rabbi Binder says, that it's impossible –'

'Sure it's impossible. That stuff's all bull. To have a baby you gotta get laid,' Itzie theologized. 'Mary hadda get laid.'

'That's what Binder says: "The only way a woman can have a baby is to have intercourse with a man."'

'He said *that*, Ozz?' For a moment it appeared that Itzie had put the theological question aside. 'He said that, intercourse?' A little curled smile shaped itself in the lower half of Itzie's face like a pink moustache. 'What you guys do, Ozz, you laugh or something?'

'I raised my hand.'

'Yeah? Whatja say?'

'That's when I asked the question.'

Itzie's face lit up. 'Whatja ask about – intercourse?'

'No, I asked the question about God, how if He could create the heaven and earth in six days, and make all the animals and the fish and the light in six days – the light especially, that's what always gets me, that He could make the light. Making fish and animals, that's pretty good –'

'That's damn good.' Itzie's appreciation was honest but unimaginative: it was as though God had just pitched a one-hitter.

'But making light . . . I mean when you think about it, it's really something,' Ozzie said. 'Anyway, I asked Binder if He could make all that in six days, and He could *pick* the six days he wanted right out of nowhere, why couldn't He let a woman have a baby without having intercourse.'

'You said intercourse, Ozz, to Binder?'

'Yeah.'

'Right in class?'

'Yeah.'

Itzie smacked the side of his head.

'I mean, no kidding around,' Ozzie said, 'that'd really be nothing. After all that other stuff, that'd practically be nothing.'

Itzie considered a moment. 'What'd Binder say?'

'He started all over again explaining how Jesus was historical and how he lived like you and me but he wasn't God. So I said I under*stood* that. What I wanted to know was different.'

What Ozzie wanted to know was always different. The first time he had wanted to know how Rabbi Binder could call the Jews 'The Chosen People' if the Declaration of Independence claimed all men to be created equal. Rabbi Binder tried to distinguish for him between political equality and spiritual legitimacy, but what Ozzie wanted to know, he insisted vehemently, was different. That was the first time his mother had to come.

Then there was the plane crash. Fifty-eight people had been killed in a plane crash at La Guardia. In studying a casualty list in the newspaper his mother had discovered among the list of those dead eight Jewish names (his grandmother had nine but she counted Miller as a Jewish name); because of the eight she said the plane crash was 'a tragedy'. During free-discussion time on Wednesday Ozzie had brought to Rabbi Binder's attention this matter of 'some of his relations' always picking out the Jewish names. Rabbi Binder had begun to explain cultural unity and some other things when Ozzie stood up at his seat and said what he wanted to know was different. Rabbi Binder insisted that he sit down and it was then that Ozzie shouted that he wished all fifty-eight were Jews. That was the second time his mother came.

'And he kept explaining about Jesus being historical, and so I kept asking him. No kidding, Itz, he was trying to make me look stupid.'

'So what he finally do?'

'Finally he starts screaming that I was deliberately simple-minded and a wise guy, and that my mother had to come, and this was the last time. And that I'd never get bar-mitzvahed if he could help it. Then, Itz, then he starts talking in that voice like a statue, real slow and deep, and he says that I better think over what I said about the Lord. He told me to go to his office and think it over.' Ozzie leaned his body towards Itzie. 'Itz, I thought it over for a solid hour, and now I'm convinced God could do it.'

Ozzie had planned to confess his latest transgression to his mother as soon as she came home from work. But it was a Friday night in November and already dark, and when Mrs Freedman came through the door she tossed off her coat, kissed Ozzie quickly on the face, and went to the kitchen table to light the three yellow candles, two for the Sabbath and one for Ozzie's father.

When his mother lit the candles she would move her two arms slowly towards her, dragging them through the air, as though persuading people whose minds were half made up. And her eyes would get glassy with tears. Even when his father was alive Ozzie remembered that her eyes had gotten glassy, so it didn't have anything to do with his dying. It had something to do with lighting the candles.

As she touched the flaming match to the unlit wick of a Sabbath candle, the phone rang, and Ozzie, standing only a foot from it, plucked it off the receiver and held it muffled to his chest. When his mother lit candles Ozzie felt there should be no noise; even breathing, if you could manage it, should be softened. Ozzie pressed the phone to his breast and watched his mother dragging whatever she was dragging, and he felt his own eyes get glassy. His mother was a round, tired, grey-haired penguin of a woman whose grey skin had begun to feel the tug of gravity and the weight of her own history. Even when she was dressed up she didn't look like a chosen person. But when she lit candles she looked like something better, like a woman who knew momentarily that God could do anything.

After a few mysterious minutes she was finished. Ozzie hung up the phone and walked to the kitchen table where she was beginning to lay the two places for the four-course Sabbath meal. He told her that she would have to see Rabbi Binder next Wednesday at four-thirty, and then he told her why. For the first time in their life together she hit Ozzie across the face with her hand.

All through the chopped liver and chicken soup part of the dinner Ozzie cried; he didn't have any appetite for the rest.

On Wednesday, in the largest of the three basement classrooms of the synagogue, Rabbi Marvin Binder, a tall, handsome, broad-shouldered man of thirty with thick strong-fibred black hair, removed his watch from his pocket and saw that it was four o'clock. At the rear of the room Yakov Blotnik, the seventy-one-year-old custodian, slowly polished the large window, mumbling to himself, unaware that it was four o'clock or six o'clock, Monday or Wednesday. To most of the students Yakov Blotnik's mumbling, along with his brown curly beard, scythe nose, and two heel-trailing black cats, made of him an object of wonder, a foreigner, a relic, towards whom they were alternately fearful and disrespectful. To Ozzie the mumbling had always seemed a monotonous, curious prayer; what made it curious was that old Blotnik had been mumbling so steadily for so many years, Ozzie suspected he had memorized the prayers and forgotten all about God.

'It is now free-discussion time,' Rabbi Binder said, 'Feel free to talk about any Jewish matter at all – religion, family, politics, sport –'

There was silence. It was a gusty, clouded November afternoon and it did not seem as though there ever was or could be a thing called baseball. So nobody this week said a word about that hero from the past, Hank Greenberg – which limited free discussion considerably.

And the soul-battering Ozzie Freedman had just received from Rabbi Binder had imposed its limitation. When it was Ozzie's turn to read aloud from the Hebrew book the rabbi had asked him petulantly why he didn't read more rapidly. He was showing no progress. Ozzie said he could read faster but that if he did he was sure not to understand what he was reading. Nevertheless, at the rabbi's repeated suggestion Ozzie tried, and showed a great talent, but in the midst of a long passage he stopped short and said he didn't understand a word he was reading, and started in again at a drag-footed pace. Then came the soul-battering.

Consequently when free-discussion time rolled around none of the students felt too free. The rabbi's invitation was answered only by the mumbling of feeble old Blotnik.

'Isn't there anything at all you would like to discuss?' Rabbi Binder asked again, looking at his watch. 'No questions or comments?'

There was a small grumble from the third row. The rabbi requested that Ozzie rise and give the rest of the class the advantage of his thought.

Ozzie rose. 'I forget it now,' he said, and sat down in his place.

Rabbi Binder advanced a seat towards Ozzie and poised himself on the edge of the desk. It was Itzie's desk and the rabbi's frame only a dagger's-length away from his face snapped him to sitting attention.

'Stand up again, Oscar,' Rabbi Binder said calmly, 'and try to assemble your thoughts.'

Ozzie stood up. All his classmates turned in their seats and watched as he gave an unconvincing scratch to his forehead.

'I can't assemble any,' he announced, and plunked himself down.

'Stand up!' Rabbi Binder advanced from Itzie's desk to the one directly in front of Ozzie; when the rabbinical back was turned Itzie gave it five-fingers off the tip of his nose, causing a small titter in the room. Rabbi Binder was too absorbed in squelching Ozzie's nonsense once and for all to bother with titters. 'Stand up, Oscar. What's your question about?'

Ozzie pulled a word out of the air. It was the handiest word. 'Religion.'

'Oh, now you remember?'

'Yes.'

'What is it?'

Trapped, Ozzie blurted the first thing that came to him. 'Why can't He make anything He wants to make!'

As Rabbi Binder prepared an answer, a final answer, Itzie ten feet behind him, raised one finger on his left hand, gestured it meaningfully towards the rabbi's back, and brought the house down.

Binder twisted quickly to see what had happened and in the midst of the commotion Ozzie shouted into the rabbi's back what he couldn't have shouted to his face. It was a loud, toneless sound that had the timbre of something stored inside for about six days.

'You don't know! You don't know anything about God!'

The rabbi spun back towards Ozzie. 'What?'

'You don't know – you don't –'

'Apologize, Oscar, apologize!' It was a threat.

'You don't –'

Rabbi Binder's hand flicked out at Ozzie's cheek. Perhaps it had only been meant to clamp the boy's mouth shut, but Ozzie ducked and the palm caught him squarely on the nose.

The blood came in a short, red spurt on to Ozzie's shirt front.

The next moment was all confusion. Ozzie screamed, 'You bastard, you bastard!' and broke for the classroom door. Rabbi Binder lurched a step backwards, as though his own blood had started flowing violently in the opposite direction, then gave a clumsy lurch forward and bolted out of the door after Ozzie. The class followed after the rabbi's huge blue-suited back, and before old Blotnik could turn from his window, the room was empty and everyone was headed full speed up the three flights leading to the roof.

If one should compare the light of day to the life of man: sunrise to birth; sunset – the dropping down over the edge – to death; then as Ozzie Freedman wiggled through the trapdoor of the synagogue roof, his feet kicking backwards bronco-style at Rabbi Binder's outstretched arms – at that moment the day was fifty years old. As a rule, fifty or fifty-five reflects accurately the age of late afternoons in November, for it is in that month, during those hours, that one's awareness of light seems no longer a matter of seeing, but of hearing: light begins clicking away. In fact, as Ozzie locked shut the trapdoor in the rabbi's face, the sharp click of the bolt into the lock might momentarily have been mistaken for the sound of the heavier grey that had just throbbed through the sky.

With all his weight Ozzie kneeled on the locked door; any instant he was certain that Rabbi Binder's shoulder would fling it open, splintering the wood into shrapnel and catapulting his body into the sky. But the door did not move and below him he heard only the rumble of feet, first loud then dim, like thunder rolling away.

A question shot through his brain. 'Can this be *me*?' For a thirteen-year-old who had just labelled his religious leader a bastard, twice, it was not an improper question.

Louder and louder the question came to him – 'Is it me? Is it me?' – until he discovered himself no longer kneeling, but racing crazily towards the edge of the roof, his eyes crying, his throat screaming, and his arms flying everywhichway as though not his own.

'Is it me? Is it me me Me ME ME? It has to be me – but is it?'

It is the question a thief must ask himself the night he jimmies open his first window, and it is said to be the question with which bridegrooms quiz themselves before the altar.

In the few wild seconds it took Ozzie's body to propel him to the edge of the roof, his self-examination began to grow fuzzy. Gazing down at the street, he became confused as to the problem beneath the question: was it, is-it-me-who-called-Binder-a-bastard? or, is-it-me-prancing-around-on-the-roof? However, the scene below settled all, for there is an instant in any action when whether it is you or somebody else is academic. The thief crams the money in his pockets and scoots out the window. The bridegroom signs the hotel register for two. And the boy on the roof finds a streetful of people gaping at him, necks stretched backwards, faces up, as though he were the ceiling of the Hayden Planetarium. Suddenly you know it's you.

'Oscar! Oscar Freedman!' A voice rose from the centre of the crowd, a voice that, could it have been seen, would have looked like the writing on scroll. 'Oscar Freedman, get down from there. Immediately!' Rabbi Binder was pointing one arm stiffly up at him; and at the end of that arm, one finger aimed menacingly. It was the attitude of a dictator, but one – eyes confessed all – whose personal valet had spit neatly in his face.

Ozzie didn't answer. Only for a blink's length did he look towards Rabbi Binder. Instead his eyes began to fit together the world beneath him, to sort out people from places, friends from enemies, participants from spectators. In little jagged starlike clusters, his friends stood around Rabbi Binder, who was still pointing. The topmost point on a star compounded not of angels but of five adolescent boys was Itzie. What a world it was, with those stars below, Rabbi Binder below . . . Ozzie, who a moment earlier hadn't been able to control his own body, started to feel the meaning of the word control: he felt Peace and he felt Power.

'Oscar Freedman, I'll give you three to come down.'

Few dictators give their subjects three to do anything; but, as always, Rabbi Binder only looked dictatorial.

'Are you ready, Oscar?'

Ozzie nodded his head yes, although he had no intention in the world – the lower one or the celestial one he'd just entered – of coming down even if Rabbi Binder should give him a million.

'All right then,' said Rabbi Binder. He ran a hand through his black Samson hair as though it were the gesture prescribed for uttering the first digit. Then, with his other hand cutting a circle out of the small piece of sky around him, he spoke. 'One!'

There was no thunder. On the contrary, at that moment, as though 'one' was the cue for which he had been waiting, the world's least thunderous person appeared on the synagogue steps. He did not so much come out the synagogue door as lean out, onto the darkening air. He clutched at the doorknob with one hand and looked up at the roof.

'Oy!'

Yakov Blotnik's old mind hobbled slowly, as if on crutches, and though he couldn't decide precisely what the boy was doing on the roof, he knew it wasn't good – that is, it wasn't-good-for-the-Jews. For Yakov Blotnik life had fractionated itself simply: things were either good-for-the-Jews or no-good-for-the-Jews.

He smacked his free hand to his in-sucked cheek, gently. 'Oy, Gut!' And then quickly as he was able, he jacked down his head and surveyed the street. There was Rabbi Binder (like a man at an auction with only three dollars in his pocket, he had just delivered a shaky 'Two!'); there were the students, and that was all. So far it wasn't-so-bad-for-the-Jews. But the boy had to come down immediately, before anybody saw. The problem: how to get the boy off the roof?

Anybody who has ever had a cat on the roof knows how to get him down. You call the fire department. Or first you call the operator and you ask her for the fire department. And the next thing there is great jamming of brakes and clanging of bells and shouting of instructions. And then the cat is off the roof. You do the same thing to get a boy off the roof.

That is, you do the same thing if you are Yakov Blotnik and you once had a cat on the roof.

When the engines, all four of them, arrived, Rabbi Binder had four times given Ozzie the count of three. The big hook-and-ladder swung around the corner and one of the firemen leaped from it, plunging headlong towards the yellow fire hydrant in front of the synagogue. With a huge wrench he began to unscrew the top nozzle. Rabbi Binder raced over to him and pulled at his shoulder.

'There's no fire . . .'

The fireman mumbled back over his shoulder and, heatedly, continued working at the nozzle.

'But there's no fire, there's no fire . . .' Binder shouted. When the fireman mumbled again, the rabbi grasped his face with both his hands and pointed it up at the roof.

To Ozzie it looked as though Rabbi Binder was trying to tug the fireman's head out of his body, like a cork from a bottle. He had to giggle at the picture they made: it was a family portrait – rabbi in black skullcap, fireman in red fire hat, and the little yellow hydrant squatting beside like a kid brother, bareheaded. From the edge of the roof Ozzie waved at the portrait, a one-handed, flapping, mocking wave; in doing it his right foot slipped from under him. Rabbi Binder covered his eyes with his hands.

Firemen work fast. Before Ozzie had even regained his balance, a big, round, yellowed net was being held on the synagogue lawn. The firemen who held it looked up at Ozzie with stern, feelingless faces.

One of the firemen turned his head towards Rabbi Binder. 'What, is the kid nuts or something?'

Rabbi Binder unpeeled his hands from his eyes, slowly, painfully, as if they were tape. Then he checked: nothing on the sidewalk, no dents in the net.

'Is he gonna jump, or what?' the fireman shouted.

In a voice not at all like a statue, Rabbi Binder finally answered. 'Yes, yes, I think so . . . He's been threatening to . . .'

Threatening to? Why, the reason he was on the roof, Ozzie remembered, was to get away; he hadn't even thought about jumping. He had just run to get away, and the truth was that he hadn't really headed for the roof as much as he'd been chased there.

'What's his name, the kid?'

'Freedman,' Rabbi Binder answered. 'Oscar Freedman.'

The fireman looked up at Ozzie. 'What is it with you, Oscar? You gonna jump, or what?'

Ozzie did not answer. Frankly, the question had just arisen.

'Look, Oscar, if you're gonna jump, jump – and if you're not gonna jump, don't jump. But don't waste our time, willya?'

Ozzie looked at the fireman and then at Rabbi Binder. He wanted to see Rabbi Binder cover his eyes one more time.

'I'm going to jump.'

And then he scampered around the edge of the roof to the corner, where there was no net below, and he flapped his arms at his sides, swishing the air and smacking his palms to his trousers on the down-beat. He began screaming like some kind of engine, 'Wheeeee . . . wheeeeee,' and leaning way out over the edge with the upper half of his body. The firemen whipped around to cover the ground with the net. Rabbi Binder mumbled a few words to somebody and covered his eyes. Everything happened quickly, jerkily, as in a silent movie. The crowd, which had arrived with the fire engines, gave out a long, Fourth-of-July fireworks oooh-aahhh. In the excitement no one had paid the crowd much heed, except, of course, Yakov Blotnik, who swung from the doorknob counting heads. 'Fier und tsvantsik . . . finf und tsvantsik . . . Oy, Gut!' It wasn't like this with the cat.

Rabbi Binder peeked through his fingers, checked the sidewalk and net. Empty. But there was Ozzie racing to the other corner. The firemen raced with him but were unable to keep up. Whenever Ozzie wanted to, he might jump and splatter himself upon the sidewalk, and by the time the firemen scooted to the spot all they could do with their net would be to cover the mess.

'Wheeeee . . . wheeeee . . .'

'Hey, Oscar,' the winded fireman yelled. 'What the hell is this, a game or something?'

'Wheeeee . . . wheeeee . . .'

'Hey, Oscar –'

But he was off now to the other corner, flapping his wings fiercely. Rabbi Binder couldn't take it any longer – the fire engines from nowhere, the screaming suicidal boy, the net. He fell to his knees, exhausted, and with his hands curled together in front of his chest like a little dome, he pleaded, 'Oscar, stop it, Oscar. Don't jump, Oscar. Please come down . . . Please don't jump.'

And further back in the crowd a single voice, a single young voice, shouted a lone word to the boy on the roof.

'Jump!'

It was Itzie. Ozzie momentarily stopped flapping.

'Go ahead, Ozz – jump!' Itzie broke off his point of the star and courageously, with the inspiration not of a wise-guy but of a disciple, stood alone. 'Jump, Ozz, jump!'

Still on his knees, his hands still curled, Rabbi Binder twisted his body back. He looked at Itzie, then, agonizingly, back to Ozzie.

'OSCAR, DON'T JUMP! PLEASE, DON'T JUMP . . . please please . . .'

'Jump!' This time it wasn't Itzie but another point of the star. By the time Mrs Freedman arrived to keep her four-thirty appointment with Rabbi Binder, the whole little upside-down heaven was shouting and pleading for Ozzie to jump, and Rabbi Binder no longer was pleading with him not to jump, but was crying into the dome of his hands.

Understandably Mrs Freedman couldn't figure out what her son was doing on the roof. So she asked.

'Ozzie, my Ozzie, what are you doing? My Ozzie, what is it?'

Ozzie stopped wheeeeeing and slowed his arms down to a cruising flap, the kind birds use in soft winds, but he did not answer. He stood against the low, clouded, darkening sky – light clicked down swiftly now, as on a small gear – flapping softly and gazing down at the small bundle of a woman who was his mother.

'What are you doing, Ozzie?' She turned towards the kneeling Rabbi Binder and rushed so close that only a paper-thickness of dusk lay between her stomach and his shoulders.

'What is my baby doing?'

Rabbi Binder gaped up at her but he too was mute. All that moved was the dome of his hands; it shook back and forth like a weak pulse.

'Rabbi, get him down! He'll kill himself. Get him down, my only baby . . .'

'I can't,' Rabbi Binder said, 'I can't . . .' and he turned his handsome head towards the crowd of boys behind him. 'It's them. Listen to them.'

And for the first time Mrs Freedman saw the crowd of boys, and she heard what they were yelling.

'He's doing it for them. He won't listen to me. It's them.' Rabbi Binder spoke like one in a trance.

'For them?'

'Yes.'

'Why for them?'

'They want him to . . .'

Mrs Freedman raised her two arms upward as though she were conducting the sky. 'For them he's doing it!' And then in a gesture older than pyramids, older than prophets and floods, her arms came slapping down to her sides. 'A martyr I have. Look!' She tilted her head to the roof. Ozzie was still flapping softly. 'My martyr.'

'Oscar, come down, *please*,' Rabbi Binder groaned.

In a startlingly even voice Mrs Freedman called to the boy on the roof. 'Ozzie, come down. Ozzie, don't be a martyr, my baby.'

As though it were a litany, Rabbi Binder repeated her words. 'Don't be a martyr, my baby. Don't be a martyr.'

'Gawhead, Ozz – *be* a Martin!' It was Itzie. 'Be a Martin, be a Martin,' and all the voices joined in singing for Martindom, whatever *it* was. 'Be a Martin, be a Martin . . .'

Somehow when you're on a roof the darker it gets the less you can hear. All Ozzie knew was that two groups wanted two new things: his friends were spirited and musical about what they wanted; his mother and the rabbi were even-toned, chanting, about what they didn't want. The rabbi's voice was without tears now and so was his mother's.

The big net stared up at Ozzie like a sightless eye. The big, clouded sky pushed down. From beneath it looked like a grey corrugated board. Suddenly, looking up into that unsympathetic sky, Ozzie realized all the strangeness of what these people, his friends, were asking: they wanted him to jump, to kill himself; they were singing about it now – it made them that happy. And there was an even greater strangeness: Rabbi Binder was on his knees, trembling. If there was a question to be asked now it was not 'Is it me?' but rather 'Is it us? . . . Is it us?'

Being on the roof, it turned out, was a serious thing. If he jumped would the singing become dancing? Would it? What would jumping stop? Yearningly, Ozzie wished he could rip open the sky, plunge his hands through, and pull out the sun; and on the sun, like a coin, would be stamped JUMP or DON'T JUMP.

Ozzie's knees rocked and sagged a little under him as though they were setting him for a dive. His arms tightened, stiffened, froze, from shoulders to fingernails. He felt as if each part of his body were going to vote as to whether he should kill himself or not – and each part as though it were independent of *him*.

The light took an unexpected click down and the new darkness, like a gag, hushed the friends singing for this and the mother and rabbi chanting for that.

Ozzie stopped counting votes, and in a curiously high voice, like one who wasn't prepared for speech, he spoke.

'Mamma?'

'Yes, Oscar.'

'Mamma, get down on your knees, like Rabbi Binder.'

'Oscar –'

'Get down on your knees,' he said, 'or I'll jump.'

Ozzie heard a whimper, then a quick rustling, and when he looked down where his mother had stood he saw the top of a head and beneath that a circle of dress. She was kneeling beside Rabbi Binder.

He spoke again. 'Everybody kneel.' There was the sound of everybody kneeling.

Ozzie looked around. With one hand he pointed towards the synagogue entrance. 'Make *him* kneel.'

There was a noise, not of kneeling, but of body-and-cloth stretching. Ozzie could hear Rabbi Binder saying in a gruff whisper, '. . . or he'll *kill* himself,' and when next he looked there was Yakov Blotnik off the doorknob and for the first time in his life upon his knees in the Gentile posture of prayer.

As for the firemen – it is not as difficult as one might imagine to hold a net taut while you are kneeling.

Ozzie looked around again: and then he called to Rabbi Binder.

'Rabbi?'

'Yes, Oscar.'

'Rabbi Binder, do you believe in God?'

'Yes.'

'Do you believe God can do Anything?' Ozzie leaned his head out into the darkness. 'Anything?'

'Oscar, I think –'

'Tell me you believe God can do Anything.'

There was a second's hesitation. Then: 'God can do Anything.'

'Tell me you believe God can make a child without intercourse.'

'He can.'

'Tell me!'

'God,' Rabbi Binder admitted, 'can make a child without intercourse.'

'Mamma, you tell me.'

'God can make a child without intercourse,' his mother said.

'Make *him* tell me.' There was no doubt who *him* was.

In a few moments Ozzie heard an old comical voice say something to the increasing darkness about God.

Next, Ozzie made everybody say it. And then he made them all say they believed in Jesus Christ – first one at a time, then all together.

When the catechizing was through it was the beginning of evening. From the street it sounded as if the boy on the roof might have sighed.

'Ozzie?' A woman's voice dared to speak. 'You'll come down now?'

There was no answer, but the woman waited, and when a voice finally did speak it was thin and crying, and exhausted as that of an old man who has just finished pulling the bells.

'Mamma, don't you see – you shouldn't hit me. He shouldn't hit me. You shouldn't hit me about God, Mamma. You should never hit anybody about God –'

'Ozzie, please come down now.'

'Promise me , promise me you'll never hit anybody about God.'

He had asked only his mother, but for some reason every one kneeling in the street promised he would never hit anybody about God.

Once again there was silence.

'I can come down now, Mamma,' the boy on the roof finally said. He turned his head both ways as though checking the traffic lights. 'Now I can come down . . .'

And he did, right into the centre of the yellow net that glowed in the evening's edge like an overgrown halo.

9. The Flashlight

William Saroyan

Next to having a revolver (which of course you could never get; which you would never really *want*; which, nevertheless, it was always pleasant to imagine you wanted more than anything else in the world), having a flashlight was a wonderful thing.

You could never have a revolver because you might make a mistake with it and kill a friend with it instead of Mr Davis, the principal of Emerson School. You might not be accurate with the thing and you might shoot off somebody's nose. Somebody nice, standing on the corner, at high noon, with his hand over where his nose had been, and your heart full of regret, and your mouth trying to say, 'Honest, Mr Wheeler, I didn't mean to shoot your nose off. I was shooting at that chicken-hawk flying over the roof of the Republican Building. I'm sorry, Mr Wheeler. I apologise.'

Or you might get bawled up, trying to take a quick second shot at the circling chicken-hawk, turn quickly, and shoot off your own nose.

It was the same with a horse, too.

Unpredictable.

A flashlight was another story.

Your sick cousin Joe's real name was Hovsep. Hovsep is Joseph in Armenian. Like yourself, Joe was eleven years old, only funnier. A month and a half younger, too. Which means that – well, you were first. You were ahead of him. You arrived a month and a half before he did.

So you went in and asked his mother how he was and tears came to her eyes, and she said, 'I don't know. The doctor's with him.'

You went out to the street, into the darkness of November, and began to walk home. You wished you had the revolver and the horse, so you could jump on the horse and go galloping over the streets, and draw the revolver, and do something swift and reckless to make Joe get better.

The whole thing was a mistake. Joe had no business being sick with the 'flu, and if he died – well, by God, you'd get even. 'If Joe dies,' you said on the way home, 'you'll get yours.' It was a clear cold night and it was the greatest time in the world to be alive, with many wonderful years of adventure ahead.

You were too busy being sore about Joe to remember how scared you were of the dark, and then all of a sudden you remembered. For a minute you were real scared, and then you pressed your thumb down on the button of the flashlight, and the light went on, and you weren't scared any more. So you flashed the light around; to the ground; up into the branches of trees; left and right; north and south. And then suddenly, as you walked, it was all over, Joe was dead, you were walking down the street alone, the years were gone, it was a night in November again many years later, and you were still sore and you still couldn't believe it. You flashed the light to the trunk of a tree and said, 'Joe?' But nobody was there. And a moment later you turned the light to the dark steps of a porch, thinking he might be sitting there, and you said, 'Joe?' But he wasn't there either.

The next day you couldn't wait to run over to Joe's during lunch hour. When the noon bell rang, you jumped out of your desk, got to the door first, got out of the building first, and began running up L Street, down San Benito Avenue, until you got tired and couldn't run any more. 'Please,' you said. 'Please don't let Joe die.' You got out the flashlight and turned it on, but they daylight was brighter than the light of the flashlight, and you could see everything, so what good was a flashlight now? You kept hurrying and flashing the light at everything, as if it were night, as if Joe was in the last night of life, and you were looking for him, and you kept asking the question: 'Joe?'

At last you got to the house and stood on the sidewalk and looked at it. Was it a house that had a dead boy in it named Joe? Was it a house full of the amazed, sorrowing mothers and fathers, grandmothers and grandfathers, great-grandmothers and great-grandfathers of Joe Hagopian, the eleven-year-old American whose family arrived seventeen years ago from Bitlis? Did the house contain the living and the dead of a tribe just cheated of its son? You went to the back door, quietly into the kitchen, and saw his mother, and you knew from her face that the light from the flashlight had found God's heart in the darkness of the November night, and in the brightness of the November day, and you knew Joe was alive, with the heart of God beating in him. And you knew that that great heart would go on beating in him all the years that had roared by your ears the night before. You knew the dead grandmothers and grandfathers were all smiling, and you didn't say anything. You just looked up at Joe's mother and smiled.

'He's all right now,' she said. 'He'll be up in a few days. Come back after school. Maybe he'll be awake.'

'Sure,' you said. 'Here, when he wakes up, give him this flashlight. He can flash it on in the night at the walls and the ceiling. Mighty fine invention.'

10. More than just the Disease

Bernard MacLaverty

As he unpacked his case Neil kept hearing his mother's voice. *Be tidy at all times, then no one can surprise you.* This was a strange house he'd come to, set in the middle of a steep terraced garden. Everything in it seemed of an unusual design; the wardrobe in which he hung his good jacket was of black lacquer with a yellow inlay of exotic birds. *A little too ornate for my taste – vulgar almost.* And pictures – there were pictures hanging everywhere, portraits, landscapes, sketches. *Dust gatherers.* The last things in his case were some comics and he laid them with his ironed and folded pyjamas on the pillow of the bottom bunk and went to join the others.

They were all sitting in the growing dark of the large front room, Michael drinking hot chocolate, Anne his sister with her legs flopped over the arm of the chair, Dr Middleton squeaking slowly back and forth in the rocking-chair while his wife moved around preparing to go out.

'Now, boys, you must be in bed by ten thirty at the latest. Anne can sit up until we come back if she wants. We'll not be far away and if anything does happen you can phone "The Seaview".' She spent some time looking in an ornamental jug for a pen to write down the number. 'I can find nothing in this house yet.'

'We don't need Anne to babysit,' said Michael. 'We're perfectly capable of looking after ourselves. Isn't that right, Neil?' Neil nodded. He didn't like Michael involving him in an argument with the rest of the family. He had to have the tact of a guest; sit on the fence yet remain Michael's friend.

'Can we not stay up as late as Anne?' asked Michael.

'Anne is fifteen years of age. Please, Michael, it's been a long day. Off to bed.'

'But Mama, Neil and I . . .'

'Michael.' The voice came from the darkness of the

rocking-chair and had enough threat in it to stop Michael. The two boys got up and went to their bedroom.

Neil lifted his pyjamas and went to the bathroom. He dressed for bed buttoning the jacket right up to his neck and went back with his clothes draped over his arm. Michael was half-dressed.

'That was quick,' he said. He bent his thin arms, flexing his biceps. 'I only wear pyjama bottoms. Steve McQueen he-man,' and he thumped his chest before climbing to the top bunk. They lay and talked and talked – about their first year at the school, how lucky they had been to have been put in the same form, who they hated most. The Crow with his black gown and beaky nose, the Moon with his pallid round face, wee Hamish with his almost mad preoccupation with ruling red lines. Once Neil had awkwardly ruled a line which showed the two bumps of his fingers protruding beyond the ruler and wee Hamish had pounced on it.

'What are these bumps? Is this a drawing of a camel, boy?' Everybody except Neil had laughed and if there was one thing he couldn't abide it was to be laughed at. A voice whispered that it was a drawing of his girlfriend's chest.

Neil talked about the Scholarship examination and the day he got his results. When he saw the fat envelope on the mat he knew his life would change – if you got the thin envelope you had failed, a fat one with coloured forms meant that you had passed. What Neil did not say was that his mother had cried, kneeling in the hallway hugging and kissing him. He had never seen anyone cry with happiness before and it worried him a bit. Nor did he repeat what she had said with her eyes shining. *Now you'll be at school with the sons of doctors and lawyers.*

Anne opened the door and hissed into the dark.

'You've got to stop talking right now. Get to sleep.' She was in a cotton nightdress which became almost transparent with the light of the hallway behind her. Neil saw her curved shape outlined to its margins. He wanted her to stay there but she slammed the door.

After that they whispered and had a farting competition. They heard Michael's father and mother come in, make tea and go to bed. It was ages before either of them slept. All the time Neil was in agonies with his itch but he did not want to scratch in case Michael should feel the shaking communicated to the top bunk.

In the morning Neil was first awake and tiptoed to the bathroom with all his clothes to get dressed. He took off his pyjama jacket and looked at himself in the mirror. Every morning he hoped that it would have miraculously disappeared overnight but it was still there crawling all over his chest and shoulders: his psoriasis – a redness with an edge as irregular as a map and the skin flaking and scumming off the top. Its pattern changed from week to week but only once had it appeared above his collar line. That week his mother had kept him off school. He turned his back on the mirror and put on a shirt, buttoning it up to the neck. He wondered if he should wear a tie to breakfast but his mother's voice had nothing to say on the subject.

Breakfast wasn't a meal like in his own house when he and his mother sat down at table and had cereal and tea and toast with sometimes a boiled egg. Here people just arrived and poured themselves cornflakes and went off to various parts of the room, or even the house, to eat them. The only still figure was the doctor himself. He sat at the corner of the table reading the *Scotsman* and drinking coffee. He wore blue running shoes and no socks and had a T-shirt on. Except for his receding M-shaped hairline he did not look at all like a doctor. In Edinburgh anytime Neil had seen him he wore a dark suit and a spotted bow-tie.

Anne came in. '*Guten Morgen, mein Papa.* Hello, Neil.' She was bright and washed with her yellow hair in a knot on the top of her head. Neil thought she was the most beautiful girl he had ever seen up close. She wore a pair of denims cut down to shorts so that there were frayed fringes about her thighs. She also had what his mother called *a figure*. She ate her cornflakes noisily and the doctor did not even raise his eyes from the paper. *Close your mouth when you're eating, please. Others have to live with you.*

'Some performance last night, eh Neil?' she said.
'Pardon?'
'Daddy, they talked till all hours.'
Her father turned a page of the paper and his hand groped out like a blind man's to find his coffee.
'Sorry,' said Neil.

'I'm only joking,' said Anne and smiled at him. He blushed because she looked directly into his eyes and smiled at him as if she liked him. He stumbled to his feet.

'Thank you for the breakfast,' he said to the room in general and went outside to the garden where Michael was sitting on the steps.

'Where did you get to? You didn't even excuse yourself from the table,' said Neil.

'I wasn't at the table, small Fry,' said Michael. He was throwing pea-sized stones into an ornamental pond at a lower level.

'One minute you were there and the next you were gone.'

'I thought it was going to get heavy.'

'What?'

'I know the signs. The way the old man reads the paper. Coming in late last night.'

'Oh.'

Neil lifted a handful of multi-coloured gravel and fed the pieces singly into his other hand and lobbed them at the pool. They made a nice plip noise.

'Watch it,' said Michael. He stilled Neil's throwing arm with his hand. 'Here comes Mrs Wan.'

'Who's she?'

An old woman in a bottle-green cardigan and baggy mouse-coloured trousers came stepping one step at a time down towards them. She wore a puce-coloured hat like a turban and, although it was high summer, a pair of men's leather gloves.

'Good morning, boys,' she said. Her voice was the most superior thing Neil had ever heard, even more so than his elocution teacher's. 'And how are you this year, Benjamin?'

'Fine. This is my friend Neil Fry.' Neil stood up and nodded. She was holding secateurs and a flat wooden basket. He knew that she would find it awkward to shake hands so he did not offer his.

'How do you do? What do you think of my garden, young man?'

'It's very good. Tidy.'

'Let's hope it remains that way throughout your stay,' she said and continued her sideways stepping down until she reached the compost heap at the bottom beyond the ornamental pool.

'Who is she?' asked Neil.

'She owns the house. Lets it to us for the whole of the summer.'

'But where does she live when you're here?'

'Up the back in a caravan. She's got ninety million cats.' Mrs Wan's puce turban threaded in and out of the flowers as she weeded and pruned. It was a dull overcast day and the wind was moving the brightly-coloured rose blooms.

'Fancy a swim?' asked Michael.

'Too cold. Anyway I told you I can't swim.'

'You don't have to swim. Just horse around. It's great.'

'Naw.'

Michael threw his whole handful of gravel chirping into the pond and went up the steps to the house.

That afternoon the shelf of cloud moved inland and the sky over the Atlantic became blue. The wind dropped and Dr Middleton observed that the mare's-tails were a good sign. The whole family went down the hundred yards to the beach, each one carrying something – a basket, a deckchair, a lilo.

'Where else in the world but Scotland would we have the beach to ourselves on a day like this?' said Mrs Middleton. The doctor agreed with a grunt. Michael got stripped to his swimming trunks and they taught Neil to play boule in the hard sand near the water. The balls were of bright grooved steel and he enjoyed trying to lob them different ways until he finally copied the doctor who showed him how to put back-spin on them. Anne wore a turquoise bikini and kept hooking her fingers beneath the elastic of her pants and snapping them out to cover more of her bottom. She did this every time she bent to pick up her boule and Neil came to watch for it. When they stopped playing Michael and his sister ran off to leap about in the breakers – large curling walls, glass-green, which nearly knocked them off their feet. From where he stood Neil could only hear their cries faintly. He went and sat down with the doctor and his wife.

'Do you not like the water?' she asked. She was lying on a sunbed gleaming with suntan oil. She had her dress rucked up beyond her knees and her shoulder straps loosened.

'No. It's too cold.'

'The only place *I'll* ever swim again is the Med,' said the doctor.

'Sissy,' said his wife, without opening her eyes. Neil lay down and tried to think of a better reason for not swimming. His mother had one friend who occasionally phoned for her to go to the Commonwealth Pool. When she really didn't feel like it there was only one excuse that seemed to work.

At tea Michael took a perverse pleasure out of telling him again and again how warm the water was and Anne innocently agreed with him.

The next day was scorching hot. Even at breakfast time they could see the heat corrugating the air above the slabbed part of the garden.

'You *must* come in for a swim today, Fry. I'm boiled already,' said Michael.

'The forecast is twenty-one degrees,' said the doctor from behind his paper. Anne whistled in appreciation.

Neil's thighs were sticking to the plastic of his chair. He said, 'My mother forgot to pack my swimming trunks. I looked yesterday.'

Mrs Middleton, in a flowing orange dressing-gown, spoke over her shoulder from the sink. 'Borrow a pair of Michael's.' Before he could stop her she had gone off with wet hands in search of extra swimming trunks.

'Couldn't be simpler,' she said, setting a navy blue pair with white side panels on the table in front of Neil.

'I'll get mine,' said Michael and dashed to his room. Anne sat opposite Neil on the Formica kitchen bench-top swinging her legs. She coaxed him to come swimming, again looking into his eyes. He looked down and away from them.

'Come on, Neil. Michael's not much fun in the water.'

'The fact is,' said Neil, 'I've got my period.'

There was a long silence and a slight rustle of the *Scotsman* as Dr Middleton looked over the top of it. Then Anne half-slid, half-vaulted off the bench and ran out. Neil heard her make funny snorts in her nose.

'That's too bad,' said the doctor and got up and went out of the room shutting the door behind him. Neil heard Anne's voice and her father's, then he heard the bedroom door shut. He folded his swimming trunks and set them on the sideboard. Mrs Middleton gave a series of little coughs and smiled at him.

'Can I help you with the dishes?' he asked. There was something not right.

'Are you sure you're well enough?' she said smiling. Neil nodded and began to lift the cups from various places in the room. She washed and he dried with a slow thoroughness.

'Neil, nobody is going to force you to swim. So you can feel quite safe.'

Michael came in with his swimming gear in a roll under his arm.

'Ready, small Fry?'

'Michael, could I have a word? Neil, could you leave those bathing trunks back in Michael's wardrobe?'

On the beach the boys lay down on the sand. Michael hadn't spoken since they left the house. He walked in front, he picked the spot, he lay down and Neil followed him. The sun was hot and again they had the beach to themselves. Neil picked up a handful of sand and examined it as he spilled it out slowly.

'I bet you there's at least one speck of gold on this beach,' he said.

'That's a bloody stupid thing to say.'

'I'll bet you there is.'

Michael rolled over turning his back. 'I can pick them.'

'What?'

'I can really pick them.'

'What do you mean?'

'I might as well have asked a girl to come away on holiday.'

Neil's fist bunched in the sand.

'What's the use of somebody who won't go in for a dip?'

'I can't, that's all.'

'My Mum says you must have a very special reason. What is it, Fry?'

Neil opened his hand and some of the damp, deeper sand remained in little segments where he had clenched it. He was almost sure Anne had laughed.

'I'm not telling you.'

'Useless bloody Mama's boy,' said Michael. He got up flinging a handful of sand at Neil and ran down to the water. Some of the sand went into Neil's eyes, making him cry. He knuckled them clear and blinked, watching Michael jump, his elbows up, as each glass wave rolled at him belly-high.

Neil shouted hopelessly towards the sea. 'That's the last time I'm getting you into the pictures.'

He walked back towards the house. He had been here a night, a day and a morning. It would be a whole week before he could get home. Right now he felt he *was* a Mama's boy. He just wanted to climb the stair and be with her behind the closed door of their house. This had been the first time in his life he had been away from her and, although he had been reluctant because of this very thing, she had insisted that he could not turn down an invitation from the doctor's family. *It will teach you how to conduct yourself in good society.*

At lunch time Michael did not speak to him but made up salad rolls and took them on to the patio. Anne and her father had gone into the village on bicycles. Neil sat at the table chewing his roll with difficulty and staring in front of him. *If there is one thing I cannot abide it's a milk bottle on the table.* Mrs Middleton was the only one left for him to talk to.

'We met Mrs Wan this morning,' he said.

'Oh did you? She's a rum bird – feeding all those cats.'

'How many has she?'

'I don't know. They're never all together at the same time. She's a Duchess, you know?'

'A real one?'

'Yes. I can't remember her title – from somewhere in England. She married some Oriental and lived in the Far East. Africa too for a time. When he died she came home. Look.' She waved her hand at all the bric-à-brac. 'Look at this.' She went to a glass-fronted cabinet and took out what looked like a lace ball. It was made of ivory and inside was another ball with just as intricately carved mandarins and elephants and palm leaves, with another one inside that again.

'The question is how did they carve the one inside. It's all one piece.'

Neil turned it over in his hands marvelling at the mystery. He handed it carefully back.

'You wouldn't want to play boule with that,' he said.

'Isn't it exquisitely delicate?'

He nodded and said, 'Thank you for the lunch. It was very nourishing.'

He wandered outside in the garden and sat for a while by the pool. It was hot and the air was full of the noise of insects and bees moving in and out the flowers. He went down to the beach and saw that his friend Michael had joined up with some other boys to play cricket. He sat down out of sight of them at the side of a sand-dune. He lay back and closed his eyes. They had laughed at him at school when he said he didn't know what l.b.w. meant. He had been given a free cricket bat but there was hardly a mark on it because he couldn't seem to hit the ball. It was so hard and came at him so fast that he was more interested in getting out of its way than playing any fancy strokes. Scholarship boys were officially known as foundationers but the boys called them 'fundies' or 'fundaments'. When he asked what it meant somebody told him to look it up in a dictionary. 'Part of body on which one sits; buttocks; anus.'

He lifted his head and listened. At first he thought it was the noise of a distant seagull but it came again and he knew it wasn't. He looked up to the top of the sand-dune and saw a kitten, its tiny black tail upright and quivering.

'Pshhh-wshhh.'

He climbed the sand and lifted it. It miaowed thinly. He stroked its head and back and felt the frail fish bones of its ribs. It purred and he carried it back to the house. He climbed the steps behind the kitchen and saw a caravan screened by a thick hedge. The door was open and he had to hold it steady with his knee before he could knock on it.

'Come in,' Mrs Wan's voice called. Neil stepped up into the van. After the bright sunlight it was gloomy inside. It smelt of old and cat. He saw Mrs Wan sitting along one wall with her feet up.

'I found this and thought maybe it was yours,' said Neil handing the cat over to her. She scolded it.

'You little monkey,' she said and smiled at Neil. 'This cat is a black sheep. He's always wandering off. Thank you, young man. It was very kind of you to take the trouble to return him.'

'It was no trouble.'

She was dressed as she had been the day before except for the gloves. Her hands were old and her fingers bristled with rings. She waved at him as he turned to go.

'Just a minute. Would you like something to drink – as a reward?' She stood up and rattled in a cupboard above the sink.

'I think tonic water is all I can offer you. Will that do?' She didn't give him a clean glass but just rinsed one for a moment under the thin trickle from the swan-neck tap at the tiny sink. She chased three cats away from the covered bench seat and waved him to sit down. Because the glass was not very clean the bubbles adhered to its sides. He saw that nothing was clean as he looked about the place. There were several tins of Kit-e-Kat opened on the draining-board and a silver fork encrusted with the stuff lay beside them. There were saucers all over the floor with milk which had evaporated in the heat leaving yellow rings. Everything was untidy. He set his glass between a pile of magazines and a marmalade pot on the table. She asked him his name and about his school and where he lived and about his father. Neil knew that his mother would call her nosey but he thought that she seemed interested in all his answers. She listened intently, blinking and staring at him with her face slightly turned as if she had a deaf ear.

'My father died a long time ago,' he said.

'And your mother?'

'She's alive.'

'And what does she do for a living?'

'She works in the cinema.'

'Oh how interesting. Is she an actress?'

'No. She just works there. With a torch. She gets me in free – for films that are suitable for me. Sometimes I take my friend Michael with me.'

'Is that the boy below?'

'Yes.'

'I thought his name was Benjamin. But how marvellous that you can see all these films free.' She clapped her ringed hands together and seemed genuinely excited. 'I used to love the cinema. The cartoons were my favourite. And the newsreels. I'll bet you're very popular when a good picture comes to town.'

'Yes I am,' said Neil and smiled and sipped his tonic.

'Let's go outside and talk. It's a shame to waste such a day in here.' Neil offered his arm as she lowered herself from the stop to the ground.

'What a polite young man.'

'That's my mother's fault.'

They sat down on the deckchairs facing the sun and she lit a cigarette, holding it between her jewelled fingers. Her face was brown and criss-crossed with wrinkles.

'Why aren't you swimming on such a day?' she asked.

Neil hesitated, then heard himself say, 'I can't. I've got a disease.'

'What is it?'

Again he paused but this old woman seemed to demand the truth.

'A thing – on my chest.'

'Let me see?' she said and leaned forward. He was amazed to find himself unbuttoning his shirt and showing her his mark. In the sunlight it didn't look so red. She scrutinized it and hummed, pursing her mouth and biting her lower lip.

'Why does it stop you bathing?'

Neil shrugged and began to button up when she stopped him.

'Let the sun at it. I'm sure it can do not harm.' He left his shirt lying open. 'When I was in Africa I worked with lepers.'

'Lepers?'

'Yes. So the sight of you doesn't worry me,' she said. 'Watch that you don't suffer from more than just the disease.'

'I don't understand.'

'It's bad enough having it without being shy about it as well.'

'Have you got leprosy now?'

'No. It's not as contagious as everybody says.'

Neil finished his tonic and lay back in the chair. The sun was bright and hot on his chest. He listened to Mrs Wan talking about leprosy, of how the lepers lost their fingers and toes, not because of the disease but because they had lost all feeling in them and they broke and damaged them without knowing. Eventually they got gangrene. Almost all the horrible things of leprosy, she said, were secondary. Suddenly he heard Michael's voice.

'Mrs Wan, Mum says could you tell her where . . .' his voice tailed off seeing Neil's chest, '. . . the cheese grater is?'

'Do you know, I think I brought it up here.' She got up and stepped slowly into the caravan. Neil closed over his shirt and began to button it. Neither boy said a word.

At tea Michael spoke to him as if they were friends again, and in bed that night it was Neil's suggestion that they go for a swim.

'Now? Are you mad?'

'They say it's warmer at night.'

'Yeah and we could make dummies in the beds like Clint Eastwood.'

'They don't *have* to look like Clint Eastwood.' They both laughed quiet sneezing laughs.

After one o'clock they dropped out of the window and ran to the beach. For almost half an hour in the pale darkness Neil thrashed and shivered. Eventually he sat down to wait in the warmer shallows, feeling the withdrawing sea hollow the sand around him. Further out, Michael whooped and rode the breakers like a shadow against their whiteness.